THE INTUITIVE IN
YOU

How to Control Your Energy Field, Heal with Energy,
Work with Angels, and More

CHRISTOPHER ALEXANDER BURFORD

THE INTUITIVE IN YOU
HOW TO CONTROL YOUR ENERGY FIELD, HEAL
WITH ENERGY, WORK WITH ANGELS, AND MORE

iUniverse books may be ordered through booksellers or by contacting:

iUniverse
1663 Liberty Drive
Bloomington, IN 47403
www.iuniverse.com
1-800-Authors (1-800-288-4677)

Because of the dynamic nature of the Internet, any web addresses or links contained in this book may have changed since publication and may no longer be valid. The views expressed in this work are solely those of the author and do not necessarily reflect the views of the publisher, and the publisher hereby disclaims any responsibility for them.

Any people depicted in stock imagery provided by Thinkstock are models, and such images are being used for illustrative purposes only. Certain stock imagery © Thinkstock.

ISBN: 978-1-5320-3194-6 (sc)
ISBN: 978-1-5320-3196-0 (hc)
ISBN: 978-1-5320-3195-3 (e)

Library of Congress Control Number: 2017916553

Print information available on the last page.

iUniverse rev. date: 03/19/2018

CONTENTS

Foreword vii
Preface ix
Introduction xiii

Chapter 1   Energy Awareness 1
Chapter 2   Mind and Body Awareness........................ 31
Chapter 3   Energy Healing 44
Chapter 4   The Intuitive Session 57
Chapter 5   Energy Self-Defense 72
Chapter 6   Remote Viewing, Distant Healing, and Astral
             Projection... 83
Chapter 7   Angels and Other Beings of the Mystic Realm .. 92
Chapter 8   Nature, Earth, and the Universe................ 106
Chapter 9   Practice Makes Perfect 113

Appendix: Exercises.. 117
Glossary... 135
Bibliography... 139
Further Reading... 141
About the Author 143

FOREWORD

Christopher Burford may be the most gifted intuitive, psychic, medium, and viewer on the planet today. Chris is a wonderful teacher who has taught me how to use my intuition and to set protective boundaries for myself. He also has been a beautiful guiding light in my life and my students' lives. I have had him teach workshops; his gentle way of helping people to wake up is always anchored in the truth that doing this work must start with loving yourself. He also has been a guide to me through tough times, always knowing when I needed him. His intuition and compassion have been a source of grace and clarity in my life.

I had the pleasure of meeting Chris at a gathering in London, Ontario, Canada. When I first saw him, I could see the light in his eyes, and I knew that I had met someone very special. Chris greeted me with a big smile and said, "You know who I am, don't you?" I smiled and laughed and said, "I do. It is so nice to meet you in person." That was several years ago. Since then, we have built a wonderful connection as teachers, radio partners, friends, and colleagues. I can say he is one of the purest, clearest people I know, and I am grateful to know him. Chris has helped me to learn to set boundaries in my life that I did not know how to hold because of childhood experiences. When I met him for the first time, that's exactly what happened; he taught me about respecting my boundaries. And when he did greet me, he created for me and showed me how to hold my boundary at a distance but at the same time to connect with the heart. His gift of being able to connect on a very deep level is something that I have not seen in anyone. He showed me how special I am. I am very blessed to call him my friend and teacher.

And now I am excited that he put his teaching and experiences into a book so people can open the doorway to their natural gifts and live in the presence of self-love and mastery.

I believe that this book will truly help people to manifest their destinies and be cocreators of harmony!

Kimmie Rose

PREFACE

My hope is that this book will allow you to learn the basics of controlling your energy field to drastically increase your personal power. After you've mastered the basics, the book then shows you how to expand your knowledge and further develop any skill imaginable. You have these abilities, and as you work on the exercises in the first chapter, you will begin to discover your skills and power.

My motivation in writing this book is to fulfill my own need to master the principles discussed throughout the book. I have chosen to write to support my own healing process and to thrive. Sharing this knowledge so others will benefit is my vision. Any students of my workshops will attest to the effectiveness of these tools. My intention is to enable people to realize that the divine is within. On my path, I have learned to trust a greater power, and this has made all the difference for my well-being.

Although I'd had many experiences in my early life that allowed me to trust God's power, I first encountered my energy field in the late 1970s. I was seventeen and teaching sailing and canoeing with the Canadian armed forces in the Yukon, a territory in northwestern Canada, bordering Alaska. My students were Inuits, Natives, and Caucasians. At that time, violence was much more prevalent in Canadian society than it is today. In the town where we lived, young women were being attacked and raped. Royal Canadian Mounted Police were also being beaten and even killed by gangs.

After months in the bush, I came into the barracks late one night to hear my fellow instructors talking about these occurrences. As they were saying that the gangs had better not touch any of us, three female coworkers ran into the room disheveled and distraught. The women had outrun a group of Natives who were screaming about attacking them.

Twelve of us young men decided to venture out into this rough northern town in the middle of the night. At the heart of downtown, we yelled challenges to the Natives to come out and face us. We were all Caucasians from different parts of Canada. I was leading, well out in front, with another man who was the leader of a gang in Saskatoon. We were spread out for quite a distance, probably forty yards, when four hundred men or more came running out of the alleys. Suddenly, I was surrounded by forty or fifty men and cut off from my friends, with no chance of escaping. One large man picked me out. I went into a martial arts stance, ready to fight.

As the Natives circled and jeered, I called upon the High Lord's power as I'd done many times before. The crowd went quiet, and the big man was filled with terror—not just fear; there was panic in his eyes. I stood up from my crouched position and began to walk through the crowd. The Native men, who continued to shout in rage, tried to charge at me but bounced off a force field that surrounded me. At one point, I heard a scream—a man had leapt into the air and landed on this force field above me and then slid off. They couldn't touch me as I calmly and quietly walked out of the scene. I'd tapped into some higher power, and that power came to me in a real way.

When I got back to the woods near our barracks, I found ten of our group in various states of injury. Many were moaning; some were in tears. As I walked in, they looked at me in fear and shock. One of them asked, "Is that really you, Chris?" Another asked whether I was a ghost. He was certain I was not a person, as they'd assumed I was dead. Some of our group had escaped by hopping fences to elude attacking dogs. Most had been stabbed and beaten; a few were later hospitalized. This was common in the Yukon at the time.

They could see I was completely uninjured. They asked how I'd gotten out. I told them I just walked through the crowd, but they refused to believe it. One of my colleagues said, "Chris, you were way out in front of us! We backed off, and you kept walking when they attacked. There was no way you could get out of there alive!" Yet I had escaped unharmed *and* without harming any of the combatants.

In the days that followed, there were no more threats against our team, and the community settled down to its normal but still violent state.

This story is just one example of the powers your energy field holds. This power is yours to claim because it is you. Just as your hand can make a fist, you can change and shift this energy.

With these skills, I survived a traumatic youth. I paid for my own education as an engineer and trained in the metaphysical. I then began to acquire knowledge directly from the source (God, the One, or the High Lord; I use these terms interchangeably). I started to facilitate others in their awakening, and it was they who inspired me to write this book. I can guarantee, with firsthand knowledge, the skills described in these pages. Anyone who has suffered a trauma will gain solace. For many, each day is a struggle. This material will aid those seeking inner peace.

Many people told me I should write, and when I realized the larger audience I could reach through a book, I had to place my knowledge on the page. As I wrote, I became energized and passionate, and I knew that all on the planet should know these skills to better themselves, their loved ones, and their neighbors. Controlling your energy field and accomplishing the abilities described could make this planet a richer place to live and thrive.

I truly want this book to be a catalyst for the shift you dream to make.

In love,
Christopher A. Burford

INTRODUCTION

The purpose of this book is to give readers a practical knowledge and understanding of themselves. I believe we are born with innate abilities that our society grooms out of us. In playing with my own children when they were young, I realized that children can see angels, energy fields, auras, and so on. Like running, some of us are faster than others, but we all have the basic abilities described in this book.

Remote viewing, astral projection, and other higher-level skills can be learned by all. The main impediment to acquiring these abilities is fear. All things are possible, and you are limitless. You can perform everything covered in this book because you could do all of these amazing things when you were a child. I have seen the ability in all my own children and many other children I have met. When with a small child—any child—I can ask an angel into the room or change my energy field vibration and see an immediate reaction in the child; for instance, she will follow the angel around the room. You just have to relearn these abilities.

As you read this book, you may be challenged to try the activities described. This will help you understand a few of the principles I followed while writing. I believe the most important values are integrity and courage. Without integrity, all other virtues, such as kindness and love, are negated. Without the courage to try and do, new breakthroughs cannot occur. Try, do, and be honest as you work with this book. These skills will help you in all areas of your life. On these pages I give examples of how to apply the skills to real life. Some examples are intuition, general health, invigoration, caregiving, self-awareness, improved personal power, reduced anxiety, and not gathering negativity from around you. It will open you to possibilities as a medium, healer, and counselor; as a channel of the divine; and in speaking with angels and other corporeal beings. The purer your motives, the greater success you can expect.

Your safety and the safety of those around you are of utmost importance. Therefore, when attempting any of the skills in this book, ask for protection, set your safety shield with intent, and try the skill and play. The activities can be done alone or with others. Another person may enhance the experience but also may distract you. A combination of solitary and cooperative efforts will be best, and you will know when and what you need as you progress. You will learn to trust your instincts, wisdom, and intuition.

I've given examples from my own experience, and you may have similar and better ones. My experiences may help you understand the application of the skills. When I teach workshops, I open with stories from my life. The reason is twofold: (1) I want people to understand how powerful they are, and (2) I want my audience to know that I'm qualified to teach the workshop and material. There are no intuitive undergraduate and graduate programs at our universities and colleges. I prove my credentials with my stories.

I have been blessed by many teachers and friends over the years and have taken courses in healing, energistics (this draws from Qigong and many sources), meditation, breathing, psychic warfare, Reiki, and so on. I trained with masters who wish to remain anonymous. This training added to my skills in self-defense but mainly improved my self-confidence. Fifteen years ago I began teaching and discovered we all have these natural abilities. I believe I am qualified to pass on what I have learned. The real goal of this book is to open you up to your limitless potential in a real way; to allow you to dwarf any of my accomplishments.

Many of the skills in this book can affect the people around you, as working with your own energy field can affect others. Conducting an intuitive reading, a healing, remote viewing, and astral projection can all be used for good or for other purposes. This book is about using these skills with integrity and with light and the High Lord's power. You must have the express permission of the people you work with, and their highest good must be paramount.

This book is for novices, and if you progress to working professionally with these skills, it would be excellent for you to adopt a code of ethics. Protect yourself (more on this later) and those with whom you practice.

Teaching is a great responsibility, and I humbly want the world to grow in awareness. Many of my students and colleagues in the field of intuition and energy healing have benefited from my workshops. I now want to reach out to a greater audience.

I want to honor those who have been a part of my training—my mentors and coaspirers. Remote viewing connects us all, and I'm honored to connect with so many diverse people. They are from many cultures and religions across the world. These gifts are partly enhanced with teaching from Sufism, Islam, Judaism, and Christianity and from Japanese, Chinese, East Indian, and Native American cultures. Thank you to all.

I hope the following chapters are meaningful and open a whole new world for you.

CHAPTER 1

ENERGY AWARENESS

We are energy. Our energy fields surround us and bind us, and they are as much a part of us as our arms and legs. You can learn to control your energy field just as you control your hands. It can launch you on a journey to discover how to control it with intent. In the same way as you'd reach for a glass of water and pick it up to drink it, you can use, shift, and control your energy field. How you hold your energy is almost as important as drinking that glass of water.

I teach energy awareness in a small-group workshop. People come to learn something about themselves and their energy fields; they learn that they're more than just physical bodies. The workshop allows students to feel the energy of their own bodies and those of others before I tell them the knowledge of what they are feeling. This brings the teaching to them more clearly. For example, they *feel* the chakras and auras before learning about them. Working with at least two other people allows you to experience this energy by interacting with others. You can work alone or with one other, but three is ideal. In this way, you can learn to perceive the energy fields around the three of you. You can learn to *feel* your own energy field and those of others. This interaction not only shows its existence but also shows how and where you hold your energy.

I begin each workshop with stories of my own experiences, which illustrate the power of this energy and show why I'm passionate and knowledgeable about this topic. Controlling your energy field has many practical purposes, as depicted in the stories throughout this book. (Please note that I use the term energy field and energy egg

1

interchangeably, they are synonymous. Refer to the glossary at the back of the book.)

That night in the Yukon (mention in the preface), I discovered the power of energy, angels, and many other things. In that moment, I knew I was given abilities not normally possessed by humans. I believe I have been trained and given knowledge in order to teach and assist other people.

I've had many such experiences since that evening. I got in touch with this skill in a massive way when I began to work with healing energy. I learned formally about this energy and to experience the mystic realm. I grew in knowledge and began to control my energy with greater mastery and intent. And I learned I wasn't the only one with these powers and that everyone has the right to own his or her personal energy power. We all have this ability—and more.

I've since trained and learned to use my intuitive mystical abilities to help people with self-defense issues, from those with close associations with the occult, demons, and dark forces to those with personal-space issues. Other therapists use this to help clients release negative issues and keep themselves from taking on unnecessary energy. Energy awareness can help everyone.

The energy awareness fundamentals that I demonstrate are our primary building blocks. Energy is the essence of what we are, the essence of our souls. The Sufis, North American shamans, Shaolin monks, and people such as Usui, Jesus Christ, and Buddha discovered the same truth about the fundamental way that energy flows through our bodies at our basic level. We all need to understand this pure truth. We all can have stories that will become less amazing as it becomes commonplace for humankind to experience higher levels of consciousness and awareness.

In this chapter, I'll describe the basics of my energy awareness workshop, the first-level workshop leading to more advanced workshops in healing and self-defense. Many of my clients are massage therapists, reflexologists, and other healing practitioners. A workshop can be tailored to any group, whether its focus has a healing slant or centers on self-defense.

Let's begin with the basics.

CHAKRAS

Wise humans in the East long ago discovered fundamental truths of how our energy fields are made up. It's also what I "see" in my mind's eye when I scan a client's body during a healing session. After you have practiced the skills in this chapter, you will acquire the skill to see; everyone will progress at different rates. You will first feel the energy, and later the gift of seeing in the mind's eye will come. Seeing in this fashion involves allowing what seems like your imagination to flow, but it is the energy and aura around you, not your imagination. Once you feel where an aura is, then later you will see it and know it is real. The mind can assist you but also can get in the way. This is not so much an intellectual exercise as an allowing, faithful divine practice—to allow your innate divinity (God-empowered self) to work.

All the chakras are lined up vertically in the centers of our bodies. These chakra points are really two cones of spiraling energy that touch at the center of the chakra. The colors of the chakras follow the colors of the rainbow—refracted light. A chakra is an energy center with a specific purpose. The purpose is based on a level of awareness associated with its vertical placement. Those lower down deal more with basic motivations, and those higher up deal with self-actualization—instincts to intellect. The organs obtain energy from the nearby chakra and relate to each other. For instance, the brain, being the enlightened organ, is associated with the higher chakras, and the reproductive organs are associated with the lowest. These energy centers power the organs nearby, while aiding the lymph, circulatory, and nervous systems. All are also influenced by the earth and sky energy flow. Please refer to the diagrams below that illustrate the chakras.

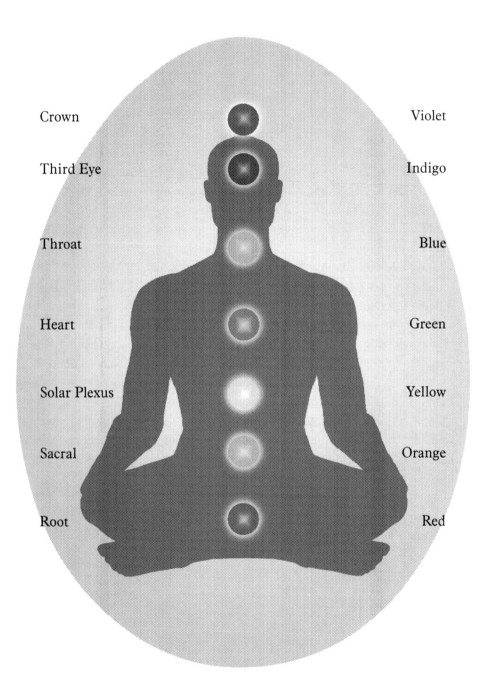

Crown

Third Eye

Throat

Heart

Solar Plexus

Sacral

Root

Violet

Indigo

Blue

Green

Yellow

Orange

Red

The energy egg, front view, with chakra points

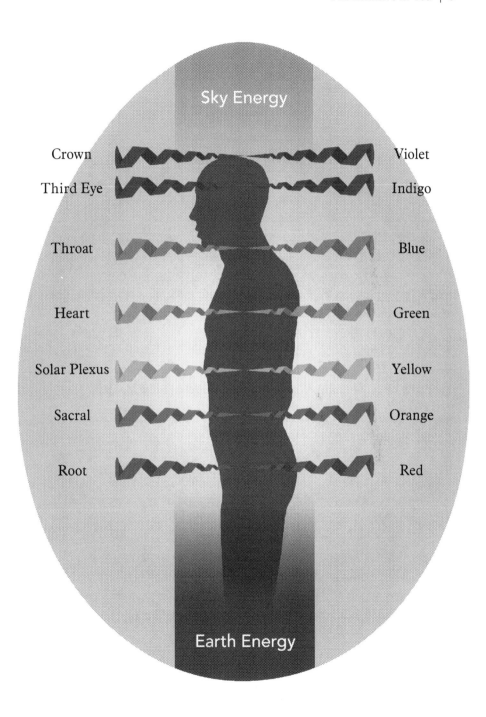

The chakras, side view, showing spiraling cones

THE ROOT CHAKRA

We begin with the root chakra, which is red. The root chakra is located low in the torso. The rear cone exits at the rear near the sacrum and the front between the genitals and the anus. The root chakra is connected directly with an energy beam from the earth. This is where energy enters and leaves from the earth; this is how we're attached to the earth. This chakra is red because the core of the earth is red. The energy comes from Mother Earth. At a fundamental level, Mother Earth is a beam of energy that fires up from the center of the earth, entering our bodies through the root chakra.

Energy flows both in and out of the root chakra; it's both an energy port (outlet) and an energy gate (inlet). We generally release blockages through the root chakra, yet life-giving force travels upward. When people feel ungrounded or want to be grounded, it's because their root chakras don't feel attached to the earth.

The root is the survival chakra. Marriage, the desire to procreate, children, finances, and security all reside here. A job loss or financial issues can affect the root. If you feel you have issues here, walk in the woods or sit on the ground, and feel that energy flow up through your root chakra. Whatever the issue, this will help.

THE SACRAL CHAKRA

The next chakra up the body is the sacral chakra, located between the central lumbar area in the back and just below the navel in the front. It's the power center of your energy field. The sacral chakra is orange. Some people call it the sexual chakra, but I prefer to call it the power chakra. It's the energy center of our beings, where sky energy and earth energy meet when we are in a relaxed state. This particular chakra is where our personal power radiates out into our energy fields. It's our power at a primordial level.

The urge to fight, protect, and stand your ground is here, as is the power to provide for yourself and your loved ones, your right to exist, and the desire for a place in this world where you have sway over the decisions that affect you personally. You begin to define who you are on an energy level. This chakra is primarily an energy port, giving off energy to the outside world, empowering your seven auras and energy egg.

THE SOLAR PLEXUS CHAKRA

The next chakra is the solar plexus, located at the stomach. It's yellow and is the emotional energy chakra. Emotional centers in our minds focus easily here. You feel fear mainly in your stomach. When you're afraid, you may hold your stomach as a reaction because your solar plexus chakra is acting up. This is because this chakra is mainly a receptor, an energy gate. It *can* send out energy, but it mainly receives energy, and this is where we begin to perceive the outside world at a basic level. The solar plexus chakra is our first level of receiving and perceiving our outside world.

THE HEART CHAKRA

This chakra is located at the middle of our systems. The heart chakra is green, and it's beautiful. The heart chakra gives and receives energy on an equal basis; it's both a port and a gate. This is where we give and receive unconditional love.

The thymus is a gland partly connected to the heart chakra, and it bears special mention here. (All these energy centers affect and are affected by glands and organs.) The thymus is believed to be the center of the immune system. The thymus is also where we hear angels speak to us. To hear angels and guides, you must open up the heart chakra, the thymus in particular. Here, you'll start to receive messages from these beings and boost your immune system at the same time. (More on the thymus when we discuss energy flow, below.)

THE THROAT CHAKRA

The throat chakra, the blue chakra, is next. This is the center of self-expression, where you express and send out meaningful energy. It's a port, though you can also receive a lot of energy here. Things that you want to say but get stuck in your throat can create issues here. This is the point where you get into higher vibrations of energy and therefore communication.

The throat chakra (along with the third-eye chakra) is where you channel spiritual entities. Opening the throat chakra can allow you to channel your angels and guides. Opening this chakra also will allow you to speak to angels.

The Third-Eye Chakra

The third-eye chakra is indigo. (The colors of the throat, third-eye, and crown chakras are blue, indigo, and violet—similar colors, as the chakras themselves are physically close and more difficult to distinguish.) The mind is a very powerful part of you, and the third-eye chakra is where you start to explore the mystic realm. Here, you become extremely aware of yourself, of your mental and spiritual capacity.

You give and receive a lot through the third-eye energy center, but mainly it's a receiver, a gate, from the outside world. Here, you receive and contemplate input. If fear starts here, your solar plexus may act up. If power starts here, you may initiate a sacral shift. The third-eye chakra can cause much shifting in all the chakras. Meditation is a powerful tool to align this energy center.

The Crown Chakra

The crown chakra is violet and resides at the top of the head, with front and rear very close to each other. This is where we receive energy from heaven, which comes down and enters our bodies through this chakra. This is where we can completely enlighten ourselves and self-actualize. This is where the High Lord's (Father Sky's) energy enters our bodies. The shaft of light from the universe drives down to strike the energy shaft coming up from earth at the sacral chakra. These shafts give life, and all life is a point where earth and heaven energy meet.

In a nutshell, these are the chakras. The colors progress from red to violet. The root, heart, and crown are equally ports and gates; sacral and throat are mainly ports; the solar plexus and third-eye chakras act mainly as gates—a balance. Energy awareness deals mostly with the root, sacral, and crown, but all are vitally important for balance. The best defense (as in my story) is when all of your chakras are aligned and balanced, though a protective force field can be set up at any time. All chakras are important in self-defense, the heart chakra surprisingly so. This is also true in proper energy awareness and healing.

Note: These observations explain how energy functions at a basic level. Reducing Mother Earth to a red beam and the High Lord to a white beam is just one side of each duality. The other part of this duality is Mother Earth's unconditional love, which is nurturing and almost infinite in complexity, as well as the High Lord's infinity. The beauty with the fundamental control of your energy field is that you can experience these two beings and all energy with greater clarity and awareness.

OUR ENERGY FIELDS AND GRAVITY

Energy enters our energy egg from the earth. A beam of red energy drives up and strikes our root chakra. Sky energy, a beam of white-light energy, descends and hits our crown chakras. This shaft of energy is the energy core stream. Interwoven with this are two other beams, explained further below, making up the energy core stream. The sacral chakra beams energy out, front and back, on a continuous basis. This basic form of energizing supports many functions and phenomena that we experience. The main beam that moves through us is gravity. We can move up and down this pole of energy. This energy core stream is also where our life forces and power come from. Scientists have theories about gravity, but we can understand it as energy workers do. This knowledge explains the phenomenon that astronauts experience when far above the earth. Astronauts returning from space travel are far too weak, more so than weightlessness can explain. Their struggle is due to the lessening of their connection to earth through the root chakra. Indeed, to travel at high speeds and great distance through space, we need to meld science with this energy and take some of the earth's essence into the spacecraft to travel effectively and stay strong.

If you cleanse your body with a dietary detox, you could energize your root chakra so much that you could find it hard to be grounded, and you might levitate! During an intensive dietary cleanse one winter, I was walking with two men across an ice-covered area with boots that had antislip nubs on the soles, while the other men's boots did not. After a few minutes of walking, I was not keeping up with them because I couldn't get any traction. I was walking and slipping. Given that the others did not slip, I realized I was actually *levitating* slightly up the energy pole. Levitation is also possible through use of energy crystals.

THE ENERGY EGG AND AURAS

A set of auras encircles our bodies, creating an "egg" in which we reside, protecting us from outside energies. Energies from earth and sky strike the energy egg before they touch our chakras, and they energize the egg and all the auras before that energy encounters our physical bodies. There are seven auras; the seventh is the outer layer of our energy egg. It normally rests just beyond the reach of our outstretched arms and our outstretched feet, with our toes pointed. The seventh aura is thin yet strong and can be made impermeable. It is an outer crust that can be as thin as aluminum foil or up to six inches thick, depending on how you are holding your egg and for what purpose. (Some people diffuse this outer area as a form of defense, making it thicker. Thicker is not necessarily stronger, and people who do this can be coached and taught to tighten it.)

A student in one of my workshops held her aura far out from her body, and the outer aura was extremely thick—three to four feet. Specifically, the outer edge of her energy egg was twenty feet from her physical body, with the last three feet being the thickness of her seventh aura. I used intuition to assess that she had fear issues, and when I shared that with her, I encouraged her to try a different technique. I asked her to pull it in tighter and then solidify the outer edge. She did this quickly by breathing and asking the divine for guidance, and immediately she saw it was more effective. She had developed a habit of holding the energy far out and thickening it all as a defense, but it was not as effective.

Conversely, I had a student who held her energy tight against her body. Only her sixth and seventh auras were outside her physical body. This was excellent for self-defense but closed her off from others. She managed to push it out from her and opened up possibilities. Her face brightened as she embraced more energy, and her field relaxed.

At all times, energy flows through our bodies, as required for health and balance and to compensate for stressors.

ENERGY BEAMS

From extensive work in healing and intuitively reading people, I began to receive knowledge of these beams from the divine. I had a client who was quite ill with overt flulike symptoms; she had suffered for months. I clearly perceived in my mind's eye two energy beams that were misaligned in her. I then used remote viewing to see the beams that were in me. Mine were in a healthy alignment. I used healing techniques to align the streams, and she was immediately well—all the symptoms left in a moment.

These two beams are superimposed on and interwoven into main energy core beams. One flows up, and the other flows down. The descending one flows into the crown chakra, down the right side of the brain, while another flows up the left side of the head. The beams cross at the thymus. The one flowing down is now on your left side and passes the descending colon, out through your left leg. The beam on your right side has come up your right leg, past the ascending colon on the right side of your body to cross over at the thymus, and flows out the left side of your head.

The beam that flows out your left foot came in from the right side of your head and is associated with your femininity, creativity, and emotional expression. It is the energy beam that captures issues to release them to earth, and most leave down this stream. This beam is where messages come most readily from the One, and the connection with the sky energy is prevalent.

The beam that flows up your right foot and crosses over at the thymus to your left brain is associated with the masculine, analytical, logical, and calculating side of you. This beam can release energy to the sky but is mainly about receiving support from Mother Earth. This link to Mother is why psychic attacks are felt most readily on the left side of the brain or head.

The fact that the two beams cross at the thymus is significant. The thymus is the center of the immune system, and with these two powerful beams crossing at this point, it energizes the body's immune system and function. The two beams are a part of your energy core (interwoven with the main shaft of energy) and are linked to your autoimmune system. A person in ill health should work on the thymus and align the beams, shifting them to pass through the thymus (see diagram below). If you cannot see energy, then add energy to the thymus, asking the divine for alignment. It will come, and you will feel it align. Work on aligning these beams in yourself when meditating, self-healing, or working on another person.

Since these beams are closely linked to the thymus, they are significant in working with angels. Seeing and speaking with angels will be greatly aided by energizing these two streams of energy. Messages from angels generally flow down the left side of the head, and speaking to angels flows up the right-sided beam.

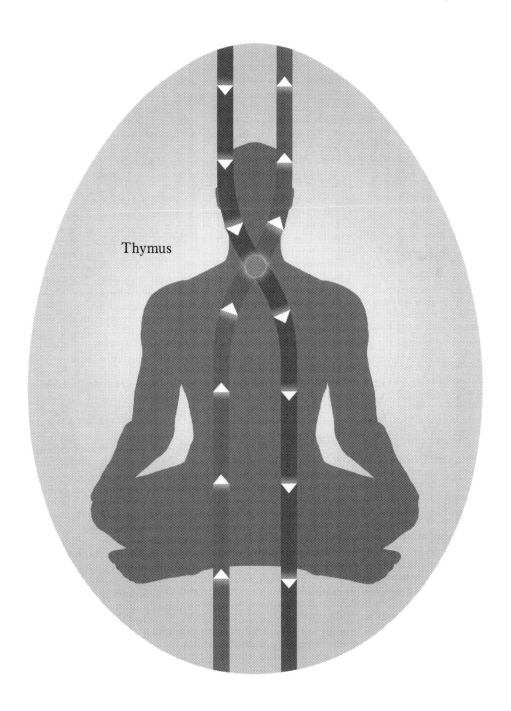

Thymus

Egg with two beams at the energy core

AURAS

A beam of red earth energy travels up and strikes the seventh aura and then your root chakra. Sky energy, a beam of white light energy, moves down, striking your seventh aura and hitting your crown chakra. The sacral chakra beams energy out front and back on a continuous basis. The energy egg is powered by your sacral chakra but also by sky and earth energies.

The outer or seventh aura is your outer crust, your first defense against the outside world. Auras six down through one have varying uses. Each carries its own magic. Below is what I have discovered over the years through my healing practice, intuition, and angels (and, of course, the One).

THE FIRST AURA

The first aura resides inside the physical body. It surrounds the organs and the epicenters of the chakras. It helps to link the chakras, aiding the communication between them. Through this aura the instinctive links are present, and an issue at one chakra is transmitted to the others. For instance, fear that registers in the brain via the eyes seeing danger is transmitted to the chakras, even before adrenaline is released. Another example would be when you feel attraction to someone in your groin, which would then be sent up to other chakras before arousal registers. The speed of interaction is fast, since it is energy, as compared to the other responses that are chemical and biological.

The first aura protects and shields the organs and chakra centers. It is most affiliated with the root and crown chakras and encompasses all the chakras closely. It is both instinctive and intellectual. Each aura is a duality and seems complex at first, but as you delve into exploring the aura further, you will see its purity and simplicity. It is the last energy defense for your core, the organs and chakra epicenters.

THE SECOND AURA

The second aura resides just outside the physical body. It is the aura that is most easily seen, as it is energized by our physical bodies. This aura protects the physical body. Skin, muscle, and even bone issues can be improved by energizing (or healing) your second aura.

Mainly related to the third eye and sacral chakras; self-actualization is a large part of this aura. Much of who you are as a person is expressed here. Issues with self-esteem, how others view you, and personal power reside here.

THE THIRD AURA

The third aura resides midway between the shoulder and the elbow. This aura also relates to self-actualization, except with a differing duality. It is most affiliated to the throat and solar plexus chakras. This chakra perceives the outside world instinctively through its relationship to the solar plexus and reacts quickly to perceived danger, clenching down on the second and first auras quickly for defense. Yet it is ready to stand firm, express power, and assert your position, due to its tie to the throat chakra. This aura is most easily seen when the person is frightened and ready for conflict, and because it clenches, it can be mistaken for the second aura in times of stress.

THE FOURTH AURA

The fourth aura is at the elbow, with the arm outstretched and the knee at its bottom. This is the central aura, connected most readily to the heart chakra. Issues of the heart are felt here and expressed here. Being the central aura, it binds and harnesses all the auras closely to the energy core. For defense, it forms a buttress for any attack, yet it is about unconditional love—love being a key to energy self-defense. The duality of this aura amazes me, and it is here, with the heart chakra, that my self-defense was so strong in my experience in the Yukon, mentioned in the preface; love supported my auras, making my energy field strong.

THE FIFTH AURA

The fifth aura resides midway between the elbows and wrists, knees, and ankles at the bottom. As with the third aura, the fifth is affiliated with the throat and solar plexus chakras. Being outside the fourth aura, love is most easily expressed here and displayed for the world to see. As you reach to hug a loved one, he or she will begin to feel love as you draw him or her through this aura. When your bodies push together, the aura encompasses the other's physical body, wrapping him or her in the aura, in your love. Because it is perhaps less responsible for defense than other auras, tenderness and vulnerability can be shown and given. When I work on clients during a healing session—and on the fifth aura in particular—I hear music.

THE SIXTH AURA

The sixth aura resides at the center of your outstretched hands and feet, as if you were relaxed and lying down, with your extremities making a snow angel-type design. It is a powerful aura, as the hands and feet can empower it directly, and it empowers them in return. Much creativity and artistry reside in the aura connected to the third eye and sacral chakras, yet the duality exists, as in all the auras, that this is a powerful aura in self-defense.

The practice of hard martial arts resides strongly here, where the hands defend and attack, as with the feet. An extremely physical aura, like the second, it is closer to the outside world, and its response to stimulus is more dramatic. This chakra can create or destroy, as our hands can, and it can hold firm and run toward or away, as our feet do. Explore this aura with its related chakras (and therefore, body parts) for more insight. Being directly behind the seventh or outer aura, it is a key support for this outer shell of your energy egg.

THE SEVENTH AURA

The seventh aura resides four to eight inches beyond your outstretched fingers and toes. Affiliated mainly with the root and crown chakras, it protects all your body systems and is your outer shell to the world. All chakras empower this aura, though mainly the root, sacral, and crown. It is almost exclusively for defense, yet the duality is that of love—unconditional love for the world, universe, and all of creation. Your divine right to have this space was given to you, and this aura defines that space.

For energy awareness, the seventh aura is the main focus. This aura is given power from our sacral chakra and sky and earth energies. We can control how we hold our auras. How and where we hold the seventh aura is important. This outer aura that shapes our energy egg can expand and contract astronomically. People who attend my workshops are generally therapists—powerful people with big hearts. These loving, kind people usually hold their eggs (their seventh aura) far out from their physical bodies. I have trained long enough to see people's auras readily, and with time, you can too. As you practice the skills in this chapter, this will come to you. One young therapist tended to hold her outer aura incredibly tight to her body at all times. Neither way is right or wrong. Both ways of holding your energy egg are powerful. The important thing is to be aware of it, and learn to control it. Just as your arm is yours to control, so is your energy egg. You control how you hold it.

Holding your energy in tight at all times means your energy egg doesn't embrace people around you or your surroundings. This can be useful at times but can close you off from the outside world, so use it sparingly. A walk through virgin forest is different; if you allow your energy to fly out as far as you will, you can feel the trees and flowers brush your outer aura. When you're with loved ones in your home, where you're safe, you can encompass their energy eggs and physical bodies with your egg. Loving energy can wrap those in your presence.

There are reasons for *not* holding your egg far out from your physical body. Consider a story about this:

I was traveling on a bus with my children to a large city in southwestern Ontario. I had a huge energy egg; my outer aura was far out from me. People at the back of the bus, where we sat, could feel the love. Others came back to sit near the love energy. I didn't realize that my egg also went *outside* the bus.

When we came to a major intersection, my outer aura went through the energy of a particular individual, who happened to be a male pedophile. (I knew this due to my own attuned intuition and many readings I've conducted.) The impact was great. I came in touch with a soul that was abused, self-abusing, hurting, and in absolute agony, terror, and pain. This was the foulest energy with which I'd ever come in contact.

I became aware of how I was holding my energy outside the bus. I pulled it in.

This is an extreme example that demonstrates the need for awareness, and it was a powerful lesson on many levels. By holding my egg far out, anyone's energy could pass through. In that particular setting, it wasn't desirable. If I hold my energy twenty feet out, and I'm walking down a street in Toronto, all the people walking down the street will be going through my outer auras. Do I want that? Do I want those people walking through me?

For another example, think of a person in an office under a great deal of stress, who really wants to be left alone in private. If I hold my egg out far enough to envelop him, does that really honor him as a person? He may not *want* my energy. Yet we also don't want to stand off when we *are* wanted. If I hold my energy in tight, is that healthy?

Learning to control your egg will assist you as your day progresses, as you adapt to changes in situations and environments. Controlling with intent and responsibility is most desirable. When I conduct a healing session, I change how I hold my auras throughout the session. If the client is releasing, I hold it in tight until after the release (refer to healing in chapter 3).

With proper control, you'll be stronger and healthier at the end of the day. This energy will make you more effective in all areas of your life. Learning how to shift your outer aura so you can blend in with the background is intriguing. When I walk through the woods and don't want to disturb the squirrels and birds, I shift my aura to be in sync and in vibration with the forest. With it either pulled in or out, I want to experience the nature trail without upsetting its balance. Thus, I can walk down the path, and the chipmunks won't know I'm there, or perhaps the fox will come to see who I am because she's interested. All this is possible for you and will come in time as you work with your core energy stream, chakras, and auras. The exercises will aid you. I have students who had little knowledge of this material, but they picked it up readily. Some skills, however, will take longer than others, with students moving at an individual pace.

As you do the energy-awareness exercise below with a partner or two other people, you will learn to control your energy field—you can do this, but it will require practice. Devote a few hours to the exercise the first time; then perhaps spend two or three more one-hour sessions with the same person(s), and you will control your outer aura and energy field well. After learning control by doing the exercise, you can then experiment with various techniques and develop your own way of holding your energy. (For those working without a partner, alternate methods are presented.)

Energy Awareness (Refer to the appendix, where all exercises are explained in detail.)

You can accomplish this on your own—we all can all do this. It's been taught out of us, but it's as simple as walking. Practice works best with two or three people in a large room that's free of all furnishings. If you cannot find a partner, it will be more challenging for you, but you can do the exercises if you have a large crystal in your home, such as amethyst, or a stone that has energy that you feel by holding your hands near it and from which you feel energy in your hands while a few inches away from it. You will use the crystal for the third and fourth exercises below. As mentioned, it will take practice, and you'll need to space out the times you try your attempts at this material. Be patient. I have worked for two decades with this material, and I am still learning.

Feel the Energy

If you are just beginning and have trouble feeling energy with your hands, spread your arms out wide, and then slowly bring your hands closer until you begin to feel a pulse of energy. Pay attention as it grows in intensity until you have an energy ball between your hands. This is not a real ball, of course, but a bundle of energy that you will feel in the palms of your hands. It should feel more intense the closer your hands get together. If one person can do this and the other cannot, then the first person should hold her hands close to and outside the other. Play with the ball to get the energy flowing. Once you have played for a while, take a break and then come back to ensure you can reactivate it. Play some more, and when you readily feel it, move to the next exercise below.

Scan Chakras

Try scanning another person. Stand beside a partner with your front facing her, and place your hands on either side of your partner's body, about six inches away. Move your hands up and down vertically, following her center line, connecting the chakras to pick up or feel where the chakras are by sensing the energy pulse in the palms of your hands. Then, let your partner do the same for you. If the Feel the Energy exercise worked, this part should be easy. If it is not, go back to the Feel the Energy exercise to really ensure you feel it, and then try this one again. Go back and forth here until you have it and before moving on to the next lesson. (If you're alone, scan your own chakra points on the front of your body, alternating hands.)

Sense the Energy Egg

Stand as far away from your partner as the room will allow. Point your hands at him or her, and move closer, slowly, until you feel a shift of energy. Then stop. This is the outer edge of your partner's energy egg—the seventh aura. Notice where you are when you stop. You may be fifteen feet away or just a few inches. This is where your energy eggs touch. Switch places and repeat, and then discuss what you felt and experienced. Relax, breathe, and try it again to see if you can change the size of your egg.

If working alone, hold your hands toward your crystal and walk toward it, stopping when you feel a shift (at between three and thirty feet). This is the outer edge of your energy egg meeting the crystal.

Change Your Energy Egg

Practice pulling in and moving out your seventh aura, the edge of your energy egg. Bring in and push out energy inside your egg. Work with your loved ones, and see how you can change the way you hold your energy field. (Refer to the appendix for more detail.)

RESPONSIBLE APPLICATION

Working with your energy field will put you in touch with divinity, the divinity given to you. Using your energy field responsibly is vitally important. Integrity is absolutely necessary, especially if you desire to develop higher functions such as mediumship, remote viewing, channeling, and astral projection. At the beginning of many workshops, I say, "Sending love to someone without permission is wrong and irresponsible." For instance, if that person is a satanist priest, sending love would appear as an attack. Any energy leaving your egg to someone else must be done with permission.

I can send energy to my own children; I have their permission. If someone's inner self has already consented, then perhaps you can send energy, but if at all possible, obtain verbal consent. For example, a woman who has just found out that her husband has cancer may just need her space. I have no right to beam love at her. I can put love out and hang it on my heart chakra, right on my seventh aura, but sending it before she is ready may cause harm and does not respect her.

FURTHER ENERGY FIELD WORK

After completing the above exercises at least three times through, you can practice changing your outer aura or energy field in many settings. Try holding it far out from your body and close in. The more you practice, the more you will be able to perceive its size and the strength of the outer aura. Practice makes perfect, and using energy crystals when on your own will aid you. You are touching on your God-given divinity, and you will learn the perception required for you daily life. Trust in you.

Examples of holding your energy in different ways abound in life. Holding your energy field defensively is beneficial at family gatherings. If there's a particular relative you really don't want in your energy, pull back. Family settings are the best place to test your self-defense capabilities because relatives know your weaknesses and how to get in through your seventh aura. Office settings—performance reviews, or a boss who hounds you, or toxic coworkers—are good places to practice. Hold your energy up and block negative energy (this is explained in chapter 5, "Energy Self-Defense"). Make yourself invisible, or do whatever works for the occasion, but always respect your energy field and those of others. This energy can be used as self-defense, and it works on creatures as ferocious as bears (do not go outdoors and try this, but use it as a last resort). Animals react quite well to our power. It's more difficult to defend against humans, who have equal power.

Try shifting your aura away from your body and closer in, while strengthening your outer aura and putting up different kinds of shields—mirrors, steel, ice, whatever you think will work with a particular individual or situation (more on this in chapter 5). In a social setting, where someone is beaming anger at you and you can feel it, put a shield up. Stop that anger from affecting you. A lot of people innately do this. A crown attorney in Ontario, Canada—known as a prosecuting attorney in the United States—was in a courtroom where I had to face him over a traffic violation. The court served a small city, and all offenses were tried at one time, including a man accused of beating up seven police constables. This man had a massive build. He verbally assaulted and tried to physically intimidate the crown attorney, who was of average build. The attorney made the giant man subside with a few terse words. The energy field of this attorney was tough and resilient, an energy level like no other I have seen. He deflated the large man through energy as much as with solid assertiveness. Size did not matter; energy did.

Police have a strong outer aura, usually held tight; therapists are typically open, with inviting auras, due to their work and personality type. Therapists want to help people but may want to examine whether they are looking after themselves as practitioners.

If a client has unwanted energy, she can pull her outer aura in close and not let the negative energy in. The outer aura can be brought in to where the second aura normally resides in a relaxed state—up against the physical body. When I first meet a client for a healing session, especially if it's a woman, I hold my energy in very tight to respect her and to show her that she is safe with me. I also create space in my clinic room so clients feel safe. The miracle of energy awareness is the increased knowledge about the world and the challenge and enjoyment to work and play with this energy, to continue to learn more about how to move and control the energy egg.

This interaction and exchange between your energy field and the outside world happens all the time, but once you are aware, you can change this interaction for the betterment of all. For instance, I wouldn't walk into a nursery filled with children with my energy out unless I knew I had permission from everyone. When I walk into a room where there are children I don't know, I fill myself with light and hold in my outer aura as tightly as I can. If I'm aligned and truly in a place of love, children rush over to me because they want to be in that love. Once all the children are close, I move my egg out. The children are loving, I am loving, and we feed love to each other. That's the way we're supposed to be as human beings: loving, enlightened beings, responsible for this energy and our power.

Try this: if you have a loving home, walk around with your outer aura in tight to your body, as tight as you can make it. Observe your family. They may be confused. They may wonder what's wrong with you. In many ways, they will express that they don't feel your love. Then let it out, and you'll see the whole environment calm down.

On the other hand, in a toxic workspace, where you've been holding your energy out, pull it in. It will confuse the heck out of people who have been beaming nasty energy. In fact, some of them may become upset because they're not enjoying sending you that energy. Some negative people get caught up in sending negative energy to others and being inside others' energy eggs. When you empower your egg by pulling in and energizing it with earth and sky energy, you will remove their energy. They will become aware of a shift on some level. If they react, keep your energy and defense up, and let them deal with their issues—they are not your responsibility. They have used their own energy incorrectly, and it is a good lesson for them. You have the right to your space and energy field.

CREATING SPACE

As humans, we're able to expand our seventh auras to take on any shape. This is powerful; a therapist may expand her aura to take the shape of her room or the entire clinic. With intent, your egg can be made into any shape required, and then you can leave it there. You can choose how to use your energy. Eventually, you'll find that you do things without actually thinking; it's become a reflex. You can create a space and go out for lunch or go home for the evening, and your space still will be there in strength. You've left some of your energy in that space without lessening your energy field. You can power a room and not lower the power of your personal field.

You can create this shell around anything—around your home, for example, and even four to six feet outside of it—that defends against negative energies, such as energies from dark cults or corporations or just energies from electric interference or bad thoughts from your neighbors. You can create a shell around your car to keep thieves out. You can create, induce, and strengthen the energy field around your children. You can create a space around your office or cubicle to keep bad energies out and bring in light. You can create a safe space for yourself and your workmates or a protective shell as you walk at a job site.

An exercise to ensure your energy shells are working comes after you are confident in the previous exercises on energizing your energy egg. After practicing the lessons with others, practice on your own during your daily routine. Let's start with your car (or a room in your house). Sit in the car (or room) and energize your egg and outer aura. Now, push it out from you until it has the shape you want around the car. Say—in your mind or out loud—"Stay around my car." Get out of your car and walk thirty feet away. Then bring your egg to its natural state and energize it. Walk toward your car. Your egg should contact the shell around your car where you left it, and it should feel like when you worked with a person or the crystal. You've proved you can do it. If it didn't work, practice it again, or try doing just a chair in your house (something smaller before again trying your car).

Remember to bring in the energy from the sky and earth. If you're in an office building, you don't want to bring that energy straight up into you because it could go through many other people's spaces on lower and upper floors. In that case, just bring it in through the structure— the concrete and steel. Imagining this happening and creating it in your mind will help you to do this without cutting through other people's work areas.

I was camping with my daughter when she was quite young. I knew there was a black bear in the area; I was alerted to him. I couldn't sleep. My daughter was also having trouble sleeping (even though she never had trouble). The bear came closer to us, but he couldn't get into our site because of the defense I'd created. Then, as he tried fighting through the defensive perimeter, we relocated. If a bear wanders into an area where I've created a defense—say, at one mile—I'll get a warning that he is in my space, though I probably would hear him first! Actually, I worry more about two-legged predators (humans) when I'm out in the wilderness. I'll be warned, and if I'm sleeping, I'll wake up. (You will find that when you set a defense shell around you, any large creature walking through it will be dramatic enough to wake you. As you practice more with these skills, you will naturally acquire this ability.)

When I'm in the wilderness—canoeing or camping in northern Ontario, where there are no humans within miles—I create a shell about a mile distant from my campsite, very similar to the example with the car, only larger in scale. This is not a defensive shell; it's just a shell that will sense if anything walks through, and it will alert me. Then, within twenty feet, I create a firmer, defensive shell and then a shell perhaps just around the outside of the tent. The defensive shells are geared to keep out unwanted energies and unwanted beings.

Know that you have this power. It helps you, but you must be responsible for what you create with your energy. Realize that you're bigger than your physical body. Try using the energy in a park or wilderness first, if you can, because the energy is clearer there. With nobody around, you have a nice, clear space to work with and fine-tune it. If you're at a family gathering or in a work setting, the energies can be close and intense, and you can be strained. Practice alone, then with animals, and next with those two-legged creatures.

For further reference and to show the effectiveness of the shield, read *Psychic Warrior* by David Morehouse (detailed in the "Further Reading" section at the back of this book).

BE AWARE

There are many uses for this energy, and you can choose how to use it. If you create a space the size of your apartment, you can protect your space from negative energies in the adjacent apartments. Placing actual mirrors that face out toward the neighbors can help, but you can also use "energy mirrors." If you're in an apartment and your bed is next to a wall, be aware that unless you have incredibly good defense, the energy from the other apartment may invade your egg, and your egg will invade their space. If the neighbors have good energy, that could be fine. But if you have trouble sleeping, explore where your bed is located relative to others' energy.

It's all about being aware so you can choose. Some friends once asked me to heal their newborn daughter of ear infections. (The High Lord heals through me; I am merely a channel.) I laid my hands on the infant and told her parents she was completely healthy. (I am an energy healing practitioner.) They said she cried often at night, and nothing seemed to help. I said, "She sleeps beside your bed at night, and your bedroom has terrible energy." They confirmed that she did indeed sleep in their bedroom and that she only cried when she was in there. I found the bedroom filled with heavy, dark energy. I told them, based on my intuition, that there had been three divorces in this house, and many negative energies resided there. I brought in light and cleared the room. I asked them to continue this by praying over the space. I worked on the space two more times, and after that, the baby slept perfectly well and had no more pain.

POWER (ENERGY) CRYSTALS

In March 2008, I was honored to be the conduit for the reestablishment of the energy connection between another planet with sentient life and our own Mother Earth. (It is a long and involved story, best saved for a book devoted to extraterrestrial life.) Our Mother Earth came to the rescue when this other planet, which she called her big sister, faced an impending disaster. By sending her life-giving energy to her sister, Mother Earth saved another planet's mother. Many books have been written about our world suffering a cataclysm in the autumn of 2008, and the event between these two planets shifted that future. I used my angel work, remote viewing, and astral projection techniques.

For my part, as a channel for these two great beings to unite, the big sister gave me her planet's basic power crystals. There were three energy crystals, not actual physical substances. I could see them and sensed that they were powerful. Mother Earth told me telepathically that every planet has three base power crystals (energy crystals), and I could use the three given to me if I wished.

My intuition told me to be cautious, and I only ever used one and experimented with another. The one I used was a type of teleportation crystal, though it had many other uses when used by people from the other planet. The crystal allowed me to astral project into it, and then I was transported astrally but through a different dimension than astral projection, such that I was undetectable by other remote viewers. Another crystal I played with allowed me to enter a void. I left in fear and did not experiment further.

After a few weeks, I realized I was not to use these foreign energy (power) crystals. The crystals were for another world and another being and not for use on this planet. I gave the crystals back to the big sister. I thought I would learn no more about crystals.

Then in May 2008, while camping near a river, Mother Earth spoke to me and gave me our primary power crystal. It is octahedron (diamond) in shape, which is usually longer on one axis than the other. I was left with this crystal for a few months before the second was given and then, a year later, the third. The second crystal is a cylinder that encompasses my energy core or entire egg and reaches down into the earth. The third is a many-sided sphere; hundreds of sides change as required. All the crystals have different uses.

Be mindful that this is an extremely advanced skill and receiving the crystals may take years of practicing with your energy field, as well as improving your intuition. That said, some people may acquire the crystals sooner. I have shown them to students in advanced classes, clients, and fellow energy practitioners, who were able to receive the primary immediately, but please do not judge yourself if the timing is years away for you.

Primary Crystal

This diamond-shaped crystal will center itself over your energy core vertically and extend from the top of your energy egg to the bottom. Also, seven individual crystals will house your chakras. The two cones of energy that form the chakra with a superimposed diamond crystal are a health duality for these energy centers. It will defend you from energy attacks but is mainly for alignment of the auras and egg. The crystals will take on the color of the associated chakra after a few days or weeks, once applied.

Secondary Crystal

The levitation or defense crystal, in a relaxed state, is a cylinder around your energy core stream, shielding the main core and the two interwoven beams. When expanded to engulf the energy egg, it is an excellent form of defense. For levitation, the primary crystal locks onto your egg and body and is set in spiraling grooves in the secondary crystal interior. The secondary crystal spins, and the primary rides up the shaft to lift the egg and person. Fear is the main impediment to levitation.

Tertiary (Power) Crystal

This crystal is always spinning for me; seldom does it stop, except when placed for crystal defense. I never bring this crystal into my egg until my primary and secondary are in place. Each of the three crystals holds the same abilities for all of us, yet they are individual to the person. This crystal will naturally reside at your sacral or heart chakra and can change size dramatically. If you need personal power, set this crystal at the sacral to energize it fully, and even let the crystal expand out to your egg or the secondary crystal. This crystal is best for warding off attacks by pushing against them, since it easily flexes, expands, and contracts.

The knowledge of the three power crystals came to me from Mother Earth. She will readily give you yours to use with integrity. Once your energy core is flowing with the main shaft, and two interwoven beams are relaxed and healthy, create space and ask her for them. They are gifts, given to the pure of heart. (Refer to the Energy Crystal exercise in the appendix for details on obtaining and using them.) The terms *power crystal* and *energy crystal* are used interchangeably.

VARIATIONS

We can bring earth energy up through the root chakra and take it out through the crown, right up into our auras, and "spray" it throughout our auras. Likewise, heaven (sky) energy can move down through our crowns to the root chakra. Those two energies can coexist and mingle inside us. That is what makes every being unique. This is a point at which earth and sky energy, father and mother energy, are combined. Play with the two beams of energy interwoven with the main energy pole to understand further how energy flows. The fact that the beams cross over at the thymus is significant, as it is the center of the immune system. Explore all aspects of your energy field.

I can see the colors in energy, but most dramatic for me is light and dark. I've developed this skill over time. Your desire to create and develop these abilities means it will come to you too. Trying to force it is not always how this works. The way you move your aura is with intent but also with allowing and letting go. You need to *do* it to *know* it, but you need to know you *can* do it! It's natural for you.

I would like to explain when and how I started seeing colors, but it came subtly to me over a long period of time. The way to seeing colors, seeing energy, energy healing, intuitive readings, remote viewing, and seeing/speaking with angels all come from working daily with your energy field, being patient, and allowing these abilities to grow in you.

There are many other energy facts, but as you play and work with your energy, you'll learn things that are unique to you or meant for only you to discover. We can all do this and are *meant* to do this. The energy is what will send us to the stars in spacecraft, but this is also the energy that will bring love and peace to you.

THE COLLECTIVE

There is a global energy, where we all touch each other. We are groups of people joined together to enhance the group as a whole. Allowing yourself to connect with other positive collective energies through prayer or other means can give you strength and healing.

Allowing yourself to feel this energy can help. Increasing your awareness will give you insight into why you like or don't like particular group settings, workplaces, neighborhoods, or churches. If you're in need of defense or healing, begin by putting up an energy field of light around you. You can ask for help from people, angels, and other positive beings. Have fun as you work and play with your energy!

CHAPTER 2

MIND AND BODY AWARENESS

"Know thyself" is a maxim inscribed in the forecourt of the Temple of Apollo at Delphi, according to the Greek writer Pausanias.

Being aware of your energy is another way to say this, and it's important for self-growth. Once energy awareness is attained and developed, you can then choose how you hold it and what you do with it. Being aware of your thoughts also is crucial. A disciplined mind gives you the choice of controlling what you think and do. Your thoughts can play havoc with your energy, or they can give you peace.

MIND AWARENESS

To follow the discipline of controlling your energy egg and the flow of energy, your mind should be alert and cognizant. If you're caught up in a negative or worrying state of mind, your energy will change. Eventually, your thoughts will affect the energy of your body, and you'll have physical symptoms that lead to sickness or disease.

This is not a book on psychotherapy, but to ignore the mind as we discuss these topics would be to deny our highest energy organ—the brain. Happiness isn't possible without a mind at peace. Solid energy self-defense and all of the other applications of energy require a certain degree of focus and a healthy mind.

A cognitive approach to the mind and energy awareness will help you. Whatever issues you have in your energy field, shield yourself and shift the issue, no matter the damage. Aligning your energy field can calm and focus your mind. You may have many worries, concerns, and a life of abuse behind you, but in the moment, you can focus on the present. Spending more time focused on present thoughts can heal and train your mind.

Generally speaking, the mind is negative. The mind naturally is self-deprecating, and it takes effort to raise self-esteem. This is one reason why staying present is a challenge. We can reach the Zen-like state of no mind—a state of just being.

Self-analyzing and always asking why can be a trap. This is about intent and allowing the energy to shift and come to where you want it. The mind works in the same way because it's energy. Allow it to be free from all thought, victimizing, or tyrannizing, and it will be free to rest. Stop beating yourself up, and control your mind so you can *choose* what to think. Ask what is happening, and deal with it.

Now, I'd have gone crazy if I didn't know the why to many of my questions about life. Why do I feel this way or that way? Why does the universe work this way? Why do I think these thoughts? There is a place in time for these questions. A constant state of peace will not reside in a person whose mind is caught up with the past or worried about the future. The abuse and failures of the past are in the past. The future is ours to change and mold through choice. *Right now* is the time to control the mind and to be aware so we can choose the next thought and action.

I believe that the mind is very complex and capable of much power and that the mind has an amazing way of surviving and helping the body to survive by coping with stresses.

A trauma to the body hurts the physical body and the energy egg, but it also affects the mind. Nerves transmit the signal of pain. The mind then reacts to the pain in many ways, depending on the situation and circumstances surrounding the trauma. Was it a stranger who hurt me or a close family member? Was it an accident, or was it done intentionally? The mind can register and react at amazingly high speed.

It's impossible to be aware of the mind all the time, at each moment. Yet by working hard to be aware of slower thoughts, you will know when things move faster. If I'm constantly worrying about a situation at work and how it will lead to losing my job and the effects of unemployment, I may not work at my best, and I could bring about actually getting fired. I can change those thoughts to more positive ones and train my mind to put away the constant thought. I can catch myself judging me and putting me down. Eventually, I will catch my mind in these negative thoughts immediately and replace them with new positive thoughts.

As you train (or retrain) your mind, you'll gain control of your thoughts and power over yourself. You will do things with your mind, body, and energy that you choose to do, not because of an ingrained habit. Psychiatrist and neurologist Viktor Frankl,[1] who was in one of the worst German concentration camps during World War II, studied the effects of the situation on those interned and those who guarded them. He felt that the effects were worse for the German guards. Frankl's captors could not control his thoughts. His thoughts were free. The way he thought about the situation and his mental reactions were his to control. In his mind, he could walk through green pastures with his children and his wife. No one could take that away from him. His life had meaning.

We may not have all the answers to the workings of the mind, but the truth is that we are the only ones who can change the way we think. If we work on becoming more aware of our thoughts, it will help with energy awareness, as well as all the topics in this book.

We should fear only fear itself. Fear is a cancer that can infect a person, a workplace, a tribe, or a nation. Fear is a thought and can be worked through. The duality is that fear can drive us to great heights; balance is required. Fear is difficult to control, especially if you have a traumatic past. Fear does not need to be debilitating or to control your behavior. At the beginning of control is your energy—before thought and before your chemical and biological reactions kick in. Try to discipline yourself—make it a habit—to pull in your outer aura and energize it when faced with fear. As you practice, this will become instinctual. All your auras and chakras and your being are designed for defense, and by quickly setting your field, you can change your thoughts into a more positive direction, knowing you are set for defense and thus reducing the amount of adrenaline and other chemicals produced, based on the reaction of mind and body. With practice, this will aid you.

Personally, I use my vivid imagination to cope. Sometimes things

---

[1] Viktor Frankl, *Man's Search for Meaning* (Boston: Beacon Press, 2006).

seem like delusions, but using my mind gives me hope and a purpose. Remember—*your life has meaning.*

Some Gems to Help You with Mind Awareness

Note: This list may be long but is not exhaustive. I have them spread below with the intention that you will scan the list and will read only the ones that call to you and will ignore those that do not. Shown below is more of a brainstorming of ideas.

• **Set a vision.** Vision helps you deal with fear of future occurrences or past failures, abuse, or things you do that you loathe. See yourself in a better place without fear. Imagine what no fear feels like, and go there. Imagine what loving you feels like, and be in that future *now.* Envision a vacation or being a Jedi knight—anything that brings your mind to a better state. I keep several memories of pleasant moments ready for recalibrating my thoughts when I'm stressed. One is a pleasant meadow, another my children, another sitting drinking tea, and so on. I need a few memories ready because not just one will fit all stressful situations. Children are very good at this coping method. You have a powerful imagination, so let your mind soar to new possibilities. Your mind will feel better and more relaxed. Envision yourself healed, successful, with a good person, or whatever you want. Thoughts are powerful!

• **Help others.** When we reach out to those in need, it lifts up everyone—all of humanity. My children taught me this truth. Living totally for yourself can be destructive. We are already separated from God in this body, on this plane of existence, so why also separate from others, especially those who need us?

• **Love yourself.** Stop being your own worst enemy. Make that decision. Love even the angry, disgusted you. We all have had moments when we've acted in ways for which we are not proud. I have many. If I can love me even in those moments in the past, then when I react to something inappropriately in the present, I can still set my energy fields in love, even if I feel I don't deserve it, given my behavior.

• **Know that we all have faults.** We're all self-critical; some people even hate themselves. Accept yourself for all your faults, all your power, all your mistakes, and all your successes. I have had clients who are victims of childhood sexual abuse, and though it leaves significant damage, one theme is always present—a self-loathing and deep-seated hatred and disgust for themselves, even though they were the victims. Energy awareness, setting your field, and touching your power and divinity will greatly help here.

• **Realize that anger is normal.** Guilt also is normal. Fear is normal. Stop beating yourself up for being normal.

• **Recognize that you are whole and complete.** You have no need of anyone else but you.

• **Stop blaming.** We are human, and we react with emotion. That's fine, but if forgiveness and peace is your goal, try to stop the blaming that leads to your shame. The opposite of blaming and shame is responsibility. *They* were responsible, but blaming them hurts *me*. I am responsible for my thoughts and reactions; blaming them will not help. Take responsibility for every aspect of your life.

• **Remember that you're a survivor.** You have a basic nature that no one can change and no one *has* changed. If you were abused, the abuser did not affect your basic nature; your nature survived.

• **Own your guilt.** It is difficult to get rid of. It's innate, a product of your abuse, and it can be healthy. Just work with it. Be conscious of it, and manage it. Guilt is entrenched, but you can *be* with it. It helps with self-examination and egotism, but don't let it take control. It may be a consequence of being blamed and blaming others.

• **Choose to forgive.** You can forgive anyone at any time if you want to. Getting to the point to *want to* is the work, but forgiveness is easy. Don't forget—we were given our memories and intelligence for a good reason—but just decide to forgive for your own peace. Do it because you love you. It may take years for you to be ready to forgive, but it is entirely your choice. Don't rush this process or judge yourself for taking time with it.

- **Refuse revenge.** Revenge will not give peace, and retribution does not give absolution. Victims have no release when the perpetrator is punished. Loving your enemy will heal you. Helping those who are responsible for hurting you will give you absolution. Revenge can lead to shame.

- **Move control to you.** Just as in energy awareness, when you become responsible for your energy field, you are responsible for your action and thoughts.

- **Own your thoughts.** Even the most complex question can be simple. Where is the source of life energy, and how does it work? When you know about energy awareness and you get it, it will affect your work, home life, and self. Being aware of your thoughts, owning them, and controlling them is a simple way to stop all the mental pain and anguish.

- **Form healthy habits.** Remember—the simplest thing can be the most difficult, and old habits are hard to change. Mind awareness, like energy awareness, takes effort, and it's hard work to form healthy habits. But when you realize you're responsible entirely for your current state, then you'll begin to see the power and control you have over your world, and you can begin to effect change for the better.

- **Control your energy.** Your boss doesn't control your thoughts or how you hold your energy. It's your choice. So be responsible, be aware, and be present, and it will give you the power to choose. That power is your freedom from all oppression.

- **Use your mind.** Use your mind to work with your energy. Use your mind to heal. Use your mind to defend. Forget failures or lapses when you didn't take control of your thoughts. Stop being critical; just know you are responsible, and work on changing your thoughts and energy. Bring in angels to nurture you with intent. Heal with intent. Protect your children with your intent, your power.

- **Calm your energy fields.** If you can't control your racing thoughts, go to your energy awareness, and calm your energy fields first. The mind will follow.

• **Separate desire from addiction.** Mind awareness helps with this separation. Anything—whether it's meditation, eating right, or gambling—can become addictive. Your mind is the only thing that can distinguish when a desire has crossed into addiction.

• **Release your anger.** Anger therapy can help; controlled physical release of anger. Let yourself feel the rage as you pound an old mattress.

• **Get a hobby.** My hobbies saved me as a child and help me with stress as an adult. Any kind of activity that generates creative thinking and helps you dwell on pursuits that you wholeheartedly enjoy is healthy. Choose something to daydream about that you can drop or pick up with no pressure, no deadlines.

• **Remember that there is a higher power.** When all else fails, remember there is a High Lord (God, the One), without ego, gender, or bias—just love and pure energy with a will. Give all your fear, worry, anger, and stress over to that Being. Dump it there, knowing full well it will be looked after.

A STUDY: MAKE YOUR OWN LUCK

A California study by Richard Wiseman[2] focused on luck. People were divided into two groups—those who felt they were the luckiest people in the world and those who thought they were the unluckiest. Applicants sent in résumés to prove that they were the luckiest or unluckiest people.

Controlled tests were conducted, and empirical data was gathered. These tests were as simple as rolling the same set of dice. People who thought they were lucky rolled lucky numbers; people who thought they were unlucky rolled unlucky numbers. It was random and varied, yet controlled. Consistently, those who thought they were lucky performed extremely well, and those who thought the opposite did poorly.

---

[2] Richard Wiseman, *The Luck Factor* (London: Random House, 2003).

The conclusion of the study was that we create our own luck. Our energy creates our reality. I play many games with my twin sons that use dice. If one is having bad luck, I challenge him to pause and change his luck by refocusing. Invariably, his luck with the dice shifts immediately.

If you want to be happy, believe you are, and you will be. You control your state of mind, energy field, body, and spirit.

TRAUMA AND OTHER MENTAL ISSUES

A discussion of the mind is a massive topic, of which little is known. Anyone who claims an understanding of the mind is foolish, as we know so little about this vast organ.

Clearly, it would be destructive to tell a victim of long-term trauma, "Just think better thoughts," or to tell someone with schizophrenia to fix his brain. Trauma alone can create damage that makes positive thinking almost impossible. You can fight these thoughts. You can triumph. The worst thing you can do is turn on yourself. *You have survived*. You *will* survive, and now it is time to thrive! Conquer the fear. Fight!

Honor your coping mechanisms and replace unhealthy coping skills with healthy ones. Don't constantly dwell on your abuse or illness. Keep good, supportive people around you, and be proud of your strong nature. Walk tall. As victims, we could not escape, so we coped. Children are great at using their minds to escape. So escape, and keep a healthy imagination. Run away in your mind when life seems down. Love yourself—you are a tough survivor with a strong character. I have worked hard at self-love in my personal life; self-hate was once a better description of my thoughts. I worked hard on healing, shifting, and finding answers to this distaste I had for myself, and it was a combination of trial and error (thus, the long list of thoughts above), surrendering, knowledge, and sometimes just going on. I triumphed to a place of self-love that I still struggle with, and I use discipline to not get into the old habit of self-pity and self-hate. You can too, and acquiring the skills in this book—working with your energy and intuition—will help you to understand what a gift you are to the planet and all life. We need you here and happy.

MEDITATION

Meditation is very personal. There are different types, and I recommend finding a type that fits you and your lifestyle. Others may tell you that a certain form is the "only" way to enlightenment. Some forms believe in a disciplined approach involving physical punishment to aid concentration. I received teachings from a master who has studied every form of meditation. She forced herself to try all forms, many that did not fit her, until she realized that she could choose the form she liked best.

The goal of meditation is to get in touch with the source of universal power; to touch the Holy Spirit; to touch Father Sky and Mother Earth energies. The meditation form doesn't matter, only achieving that goal. Realize that being able to touch the source for even a microsecond is extremely beneficial. Discipline is helpful, as is surrendering and allowing. The time you need to meditate may be during a crisis situation, when you have a moment to dip into the well of light, so a quick mind assists as well.

Just like the path to enlightenment, meditation is very personal. I suggest learning different types. Perhaps you prefer a guided meditation, transcendental meditation, or learning to concentrate on one thing and focusing. You must find your own way and your path.

If you're new to meditation, try this: (Refer to the appendix for more explanation.)

- Sit in a quiet room at a quiet time.
- Do it in silence first, or try it with music.
- Focus on a ball of light at your heart or third-eye chakra, or focus on the sky or earth energy that enters your energy field
- Calm your breathing, and go into the light. Try to fill your mind with just that light.
- Feel the love, and let go of everything.
- You may shift your attention to areas of your body that require healing, but keep coming back to that well of light.

When you feel comfortable with this method, attempt it in progressively more intense situations. Vary the way and time that you meditate, and learn to dip into this light while jogging, at work, or while driving.

Or try deep-breath therapy to focus your body before you meditate. Breathe in for a count of five, hold it for a count of five, and take five more counts to let it out. Repeat this ten times, and you'll relax. Doing this on a regular basis will drop your overall anxiety and make you generally more relaxed for meditation. The mind is always in need of a rest, an emptying.

Meditations that are led by others work well for some people. I can't meditate to a led meditation yet, but I do lead meditations for clients who find it very beneficial. Find what is best for you and your mind. Realize that your style may change, and your life may change.

When I recently got back into meditation, I focused on an oak leaf. I was out on a fine autumn day, and, like a little child, I kicked leaves for an hour. The act of just kicking leaves and being a child was meditative. I looked for different leaves and put them in my pocket. I brought them home, and I pressed them, an activity I'd done with my children.

At the time I wanted to meditate, I concentrated on an oak leaf to empty my mind. I sat and focused only on the leaf. For days I used the oak leaf to guide my meditation. By having nothing but the leaf in my mind, it aided in developing a state of no mind. The leaf was something real, and my mind filled with its image until it was all that was there. Then, after doing it long enough, the leaf was constant and unchanging in my mind, and my mind eventually perceived it as nothing—no mind. That worked for me for a while, so use whatever works for you to get into your spiritual space and meditate. Use props or discipline, sound or silence (nature or man-made) to reach the state of *no mind*. Quiet your thoughts, and be aware of your mind.

Meditation can have great intensity. A friend and teacher of mine, probably the most powerful meditator I know, trained himself, through meditation, to move objects on a table. His father was a great healer, and when my friend was about eight years old, he told his father he wanted to be able to heal too. His father told him to sit in a chair and think about one thing—a leaf, a blade of grass, or a grain of sand—for two minutes. Then it was five minutes, then eight, and so on until he could do it for an hour. Only then was he ready to focus his energy and properly meditate. Then, his father taught him to heal and do many things in a very disciplined way.

Use any method that gets you to focus, and if you can truly touch the infinite (which is unity, the well of light, or the source—the divine) for even a millisecond, you have done a great deal of good for your soul. It's not about being in the well of light for hours, though that would be a great and beneficial achievement. I praise people who can do that. When you're starting out, don't worry about that kind of a goal. Just be with your thoughts. Let your thoughts come and go (and if you have an itch, scratch it). Take your time, and try to get lost in God for just a moment, and then slowly go for a longer duration without judging.

Meditation is at the core of feeding your soul and spirit. Your mind will naturally meditate to feed your soul. So don't worry; you are meditating without even knowing it. Your soul will tell you when it is time to meditate. Listen for those signals. Only you can find your path, and only you can find your best method of meditation. Research the types of meditation, or just experience it and explore it. Have fun with it. (Note: I have purposely left out discussing the different types of meditation, deciding to emphasize the personal energy field and the divine within.)

TELEKINESIS

One example of the power of the mind is telekinesis, the ability to move objects using the force of your thoughts. A mentor of mine could move large objects, which he learned by intense mind-focus techniques, including the ability to concentrate on a single point for hours at a time. I believe telekinetic ability was commonplace at a point in our ancient history, when Mother Earth's power was stronger and more prevalent.

Telekinesis is also the third-eye chakra beaming energy at the object's energy to defy gravity. When you consider that this chakra is mainly an energy gate, you'll understand the need for mind power. I know people who can cause candle flames to flicker, and this is a good starting point if you wish to train this ability.

BODY AWARENESS

The body is vital to spiritual growth. A strong body means a strong spirit (to a certain extent). The main focus of this book is intuition and spiritual/energy awareness, so I'm covering the physical body only briefly. But if you are to attain personal growth, mind, body, and spirit require equal emphasis. Physical body awareness will give you great spiritual and mental insight.

Keeping your body fit, conducting regular dietary cleanses (detoxifications—refer to Jonn Matsen's book in the "Further Reading" section of this book), walking and running in nature, developing flexibility and strength, and general physical well-being are all important for spiritual development. Though full spiritual maturity may take place in old age, a strong physique will aid you. (Please note that all aspects and skills in this book can be achieved without the use of drugs or other substances. A clean body supports all the abilities described.)

One of the best ways to develop your energy control and awareness is by exercising. Start with walking and then expand. A nature walk is a great way to practice the techniques in this book. Stay healthy and fit.

DIET

Dietary detoxification can be very beneficial for cleansing the body. As you cleanse the physical body, you will cleanse your energy field—auras, chakras, and all aspects. I highly recommend this, but I caution you to be gentle. Some of the methods of quick cleansing can be harsh on your body.

One way to ensure your good health is to pray over your food. The act of saying grace puts healthy energy into food. Scan your food as you would someone's chakra, and see how the energy feels. Have fun with this, and don't be burdened by having to fear food. Eat what feels good, and trust your instincts. You can become stressed by trying to eat natural and perfect. A good cleanse can get rid of any toxins you pick up and allow the body to heal. Our physical and energy eggs have an amazing capacity for self-healing.

When detoxing, remember that you'll release physically, emotionally, and spiritually (if you are doing it correctly), so be ready for shifts in your energy field, body, and mind. These shifts can be subtle or dramatic; pain may ease, for example. Be gentle, and stop if you feel any pain. I don't recommend using herbs to accelerate or replace a good dietary detox. Let the body have time to heal, and take the weeks required to dump that stuff. Remember toxins have been built up over decades, so why do we feel we can release them all in the first detox and in a few weeks? There is no quick fix to years of neglect.

A good source of water can't be stressed enough. Potable water is quickly becoming an expensive and scarce resource on the planet. Water has a magnetic and spiritual energy that cleanses and refreshes our bodies and energy fields. In a survival situation, water is more critical than shelter or fire. Be sure good water is a part of your diet.

Many modalities can benefit your physical health; to name a few, homeopathy, naturopathy, massage, acupuncture, chiropractic, the medical system, and many others can aid and support your body (and energy egg). Trust your intuition to find the correct support; energizing your energy field aids with intuition.

Let's all work toward replenishing our food and water resources. We are of the earth. Mother Earth can help you to discover what is healthy for your body. Connect with her, and you'll sense what you need.

A CAVEAT

Many times in life, we feel overwhelmed. If you suffer with an anxiety disorder or something more severe, it can be very difficult to think positively. Fear can overcome you, and all seems hopeless. At these times, how can you follow the suggestions in this chapter?

First, don't turn on yourself for struggling. Second, remember the most important activity you can do: pray. Third, know for certain that the High Lord can send angels, Mother Earth, energy, protection, and comfort—all you need. Bring in the energy and fill your egg with light.

In addition, you need to sleep and turn your mind off to stay healthy. What then? Does your energy egg cease to be energized and all your protection fall away? No, it does not! Know that your intent can improve your life, and energy, mind, and body awareness will become second nature with practice. The High Lord and Mother Earth will keep you. You are ultimately in their care.

CHAPTER 3

ENERGY HEALING

Everyone can heal. Everyone is a healer. The energy naturally flows from our hands. A mother who holds a baby is releasing energy into the child at all times. Everyone can make use of this power.

The energy ball you felt during the first exercise of chapter 1, called Feel the Energy, was the beginning for you as a healer. The next, called Scan Chakras, allowed you to sense the energy field in another person. These same sensitivities to the energy centers will allow you to sense blockages in healthy energy flow. To test this, scan an area of a friend or loved one that you know is bothering him—a headache, for example, or sore muscle. As you pass your hand above the injured area, sense the difference from the surrounding areas. Keep practicing this until you can sense troubled areas in others or yourself.

Now, hold your hand against the troubled area. Energy will flow from your hand into the injury. Place your other hand on the opposite side of the body part. For example, if it's a headache, the head would be held between the hands; with a knee injury, the knee is held between the hands. Now both hands will send energy into the injury, restoring healthy flow. Depending on the injury, you may need to hold in one place for twenty minutes or longer. If you feel a sudden drop off in energy flow remove your hands, and work on it again, at least four hours later. The injury may heal before twenty minutes, so stop shortly afterward; this means balance is restored. (A thorough explanation is in the appendix.)

Remember while healing to keep your energy field energized, as described in chapter 1.

It's also possible to heal at a distance, praying for or sending healing energy over time and space. This is akin to remote viewing.

We can enhance our natural gifts of healing by using different methods or initiations to open the healing channels further. If you follow this path, choose your teacher well, and choose the modality that fits you the best. Healers usually have a calling, so your teacher and methods should align with your own calling. Honor the person you work on, but also honor yourself. If you know you are not in a place to heal a particular issue in someone, suggest she see another practitioner.

Once while conducting a healing on a client, I discovered problems with the liver and recommended he see a doctor and have a blood test done. The liver was on the verge of shutting down but was caught in time. In addition, the principles we discussed in chapter 1 on how you hold your energy to honor the client and yourself must apply. Sometimes the client needs to be aware of you but not be within your energy field. When you have the knowledge of how to control your energy field, you must use it with honor and integrity at all times.

PROTECTION AND SAFETY

Protection and safety for you and the client is paramount. Your concern for the client may do harm if the healing is forced. Always respect your client's energy. You can intentionally block psychic invaders or the client's link to dark energies (someone's hate, for example). The client must feel protected and safe at all times. This is especially important if there is a history of abuse and possibly a lack of respect for her own person. Be sensitive to her needs, and discuss this before, during, and after the session, as required.

Before doing hands-on healing with a female client, I take extra time to make her comfortable by discussing the issues she is experiencing. Your client must know there is a clear line of respect for her as a person. This respect is love and pure care, and it is the basis of the healing.

PREPARING THE SPACE

When you practice as an energy healer (or other practitioner), you must first create an energetically healthy space. It must be nurturing for your client and healthy for you. If you enjoy your space, you'll work better in it. As simple as this sounds, it's not always done. Ergonomically, your healing space (table, chair, and so on) must be comfortable, but the space must also be energetically prepared. (Refer to Create Space in the appendix.)

Does the space have some negative energy from outside or past use? If so, this must be cleared. The space must have good connections to earth and sky. Keeping the space cleared will be an ongoing effort, but this will be more difficult if it's a multipurpose room. Even if it's used as living space, that will change the healing energy. Try to keep a separate area that is honored as your sacred healing space. To be clear, healing can be done in a gutter on the side of the road. But even on the side of the road, you should create a space, an egg around you and the client. It's so much more beneficial to have a dedicated, cleared space so you don't have to put energy into creating space each time.

If using a massage table (a good idea), test the table yourself so you know it's comfortable. If using a chair, ensure it is ergonomically designed. Music, candles, incense, feathers, and crystals or other items can enhance your space, but be sensitive to scents and how they could affect the healing.

PREPARING THE HEALER (YOU)

You'll want to feel centered in the room. Before the session, clear your energy field and align your chakras. Remember the session is also healing for you; you will also receive energy. You may not be completely balanced, but try to be cleared before working on the client directly.

As the healer, you are a channel of the energy, and that flow can be blocked or restricted by personal issues and ego at times. By letting go of ego, you will be able to acknowledge your weakness and hurt, clearing yourself to be available for the client. Ego is not just about how great a healer you are; it may be linked to an overwhelming desire to heal the person. Forcing a healing so you can prove your abilities is not in the patient's best interests or your own.

Practitioners must be aware that their own issues will come up, and they must be honored, healed, and released before helping the client. It's difficult to heal until you have dealt with your own issues and you've developed good self-healing techniques to quickly release your own issues before and during the session.

PREPARING THE PATIENT

Be sure the client is comfortable, warm enough, and not experiencing discomfort from physical elements. For the first session (or part of it), hold your energy in tight to your body so your outer aura doesn't touch that of the client, if possible. Then, let your aura out to touch the client's, and use your hand to sweep the auras. This allows the patient's energy to experience your energy gently and become accustomed to the experience. Wait until the connection is positive, and don't force *your* energy on the client.

THE SESSION

The session is about honoring you, the client, and the space. Healing allows clients to find their own paths to health and alignment, a path toward freeing the blocks inside. The practitioner must ensure that the shift is always gentle and at the client's speed. At times, even the patient's inner self will tell you to push, but a harsh or forced release will bring about only temporary relief. For a healer who respects the client, the client's process, the energy, and her own process, this sensitivity is possible. Healing is not manipulative; it's not about light or dark, kindness or gentleness. It's about pure energy transfer.

INITIAL ASSESSMENT

Holding your energy in tight, use your hands to scan the client's outer aura. Scan for any damage or energy blockages. As the client becomes more comfortable, let your auras touch, and then scan the physical body, keeping your hands one to two feet above the client. Talking can ease tension, creating comfort and trust.

The healing energy will come mainly from your hands, so concentrate on the hands and the areas they touch. Start at the head or feet and move to areas as you are led. The initial assessment is important, but things will shift, so scan when needed to see the shifts.

At this point, you may wish to discuss what you sense with the client. Talking through comfort issues and doing some counseling can be very beneficial for the first session. Help the client to become confident in your—and her own—ability to heal.

HANDS-ON HEALING

Shoulders, backs, and legs are easy to work on for first-time clients, but not everyone is comfortable with touch. Therefore, be aware of the client's comfort level and query the client as you proceed. It is easiest to work on someone while he or she lies clothed on a portable massage table, but you can have the client seated in a comfortable chair. You will need a stool. Ensure you are both comfortable.

Assuming you did the initial assessment, begin by placing your hands on her head (this can be over both ears or on the forehead and back of head). Leave hands on the head for a few minutes (longer if there are issues here) and then move to the feet. Place one hand on the top and the other on the bottom, back, or the ankle (your choice) of each foot. Hold this for a few minutes. Then hold both feet, one in each hand, for five minutes.

If you wish to work on the areas with issues that came up in your scan, then move to each area, placing your hands on opposite sides of the area concerned. Leave them there for five minutes (longer, if your intuition tells you to), or move off if the energy flowing out of your hands drops off. Then go to the chakra nearest to the affected area (do this with two, if both chakras are of equal distance), and place your hands on either side of the chakra, front of body and back of body. Your hands do not have to touch the person; within six inches is fine. The energy will flow through a chair or table.

Continue to work on the affected or injured areas and the associated chakras. When you are finished, place your hands on the client's head, as at the beginning, and then move to the feet and finish there, a few minutes at each spot. The person will feel relaxed and may need to lie or sit still for a while before getting up.

Alternately to working on affected areas, the person (or you) may want a general healing treatment. Perhaps no troubled areas arose during the assessment; in this case, follow the steps detailed in the appendix for a general healing treatment.

I recommend a minimum of three sessions for clients. The first session should start things moving and make the client comfortable; the second is intense; the third can begin intensely but end calmly with completion. Leave the client well-grounded after each session by checking his energy flow from earth. This can be done by feeling it in your hands, intuition, or remote viewing.

Even if you are working at a person's feet, you can use distant healing to work on other areas (more on this in chapter 6). This is also helpful (even with long-term clients who trust you) in getting at unreachable spots or to do deep organ/tissue work, where your hands simply cannot go. It is helpful to develop your remote scanning technique to the point where you can scan the person inside and out for energy blocks.

Blocks in energy will appear different for every practitioner. You may see things, feel things, or be told where the block is, so do what works for you. Personally, I see energy blocks as dark patches, where the light has difficulty passing through. I work on these areas and take time to put energy into them. It is not bad energy, and the block has probably defended the body from further damage, much like scar tissue protects inner tissues by healing quickly. Honor the block, allowing it to go when the body is ready to restructure the energy back to its natural state.

I am a proponent of very gentle releases of disease and blocks. This is a longer-lasting type of healing. I have done many forced releases on myself to forge ahead with my own healing. I needed to learn how to heal myself first before helping others to heal. Never attack an issue. It was put there for a purpose.

DAMAGE AND INJURIES

Injuries can become chronic due to emotions or spiritual issues around the injury. You don't have to understand an issue to release it. Some of the best releases I've had with clients were when I had no insight at all. It's important to let go of ego and the need to see, know, and heal everything and everyone. Yet as a healer, if I sense the emotion around the issue, I can work with the client on releasing it. This often leads to addressing the chronic nature of the wound.

When there is damage, the body is not the only affected area; all seven auras are damaged. The issue that is felt acutely in the body can actually be hurting mainly in an aura. Removing the hand from the physical body to do aura work can help release the issue. If the injury was accompanied by anger, fear, or shame, the damage can become chronic. The emotions must be healed and released to fully restore balance and health. Fascia and auras can easily hold emotion.

Scar tissue can leave chronic issues, since it is not the healthiest way to heal. However, it can be released and cleared, though the scar tissue may remain. If there is scarring on the body, then the aura is scarred; therefore, release the auras as well.

Quite often, when there is damage to a certain area or chakra, people will put up a shield or a block that defends that area. We have to honor those blockages. The person may not be ready for a shield to come down. To remove it will remove the person's only ability to defend that area. To improve the flow of energy, start from the outer auras. When those are vibrating properly, the blocks in the physical body can let go. Then, heal that area and restore proper flow. Throughout the process, honor the blocks, even if they caused disease, as they fulfilled a role for the person.

People ask me, "When I am injured, doesn't that damage me and allow negative energies to come in?" Some ask, "Could a demon enter me through the damaged area?" The body is actually amazing at healing trauma. When you are injured, it damages not just the skin and muscle but also the first aura underneath the skin and the second to the seventh. But the energy egg immediately throws up a shield, and energy scar tissue will form overnight. Little negative energy enters though the rift (and certainly no demons). Most negative energy is generated by the client's negative emotions around the injury and the injury itself. I have found, through many healing sessions, that scar tissue over those damaged areas—a scar energy in the auras—keeps your energy field intact. This scar tissue can align to allow proper energy flow without major issue.

RELEASING

Generally speaking, releasing will be in the direction of natural flow. As we discussed in chapter 1, the energy mainly flows from the crown to the root chakra. This is gravity, and the body naturally expels in that direction (the bladder and bowel expel downward). Therefore, most releases involve making sure the client is well grounded so he can release in that direction. Yet on many occasions, I've had miraculous releases through the crown and the heart chakra. You could release through any chakra. Ask the issue itself and the client's inner self how the blockage should move.

How you hold your own energy can help someone release. If I'm holding my own aura out around the person, giving her love, but she's trying to do a release, I need to pull back my energy and allow her to release through her own energy field and not through mine. In fact, some clients are so respectful that they won't release their issues through my aura.

I use many methods of releasing. Most should not be practiced by people who lack confidence. My training came from many sources and, with years behind me, I've had great success with the Holy Spirit guiding me. Reiki masters have adamantly told me to cease many of my methods, but I've used them to instantly and dramatically heal people in the moment (rather, the High Lord used me as a channel). I depend on my angels, the High Lord, and Mother Earth to direct me. The client has to be ready to release, and I must have the client's highest good in mind, being mindful that I'm at risk. Don't be afraid to be creative and follow your angels.

One technique (based in Islamic healing) involves taking illness out of others and into myself. My young children, who hadn't been sick for a year, contracted a very bad case of the flu. It was only in its second day, not yet full course. While they napped, I worked on them for twenty minutes each. I took the flu out of them into me, and then let it go out into the earth. The children were instantly healed. Many would not recommend this method due to the great risk associated with it, but this was with my own children.

When an issue like that goes through you, some of it can get trapped inside you. You must realize that it's not *your* issue. It's easier for you to release the issue because it's not yours. Once, I took the uterine cancer from a client into my body and held on to it for a while before I could get rid of it. The reason for my difficulty was my own issues around cancer; it was part of my own healing that I hung on to it. I let it go before the day ended by sending it into the earth through my core energy field. I was called to release the cancer in that way.

The energy of the cancer flows out and into you in a controlled fashion; otherwise, it will not leave the client and will go to ground easily. If there is a risk of the energy accidentally flowing elsewhere, then it will not leave the client, as the divinity of your sky and earth energy flow will not allow it. It is an extreme way of healing another and should not be practiced on a regular basis. The practitioner must be very well grounded. Of course, you should always be well grounded when you're healing but in this case *very* well grounded, so you can release the client's issue as quickly as possible.

If you take on a client's issues through any method, physical or psychosomatic, and the issue is not ready to be released, you may find that you have to give those issues back to the client. I've worked with and played with various people in support groups, and it's quite interesting to take on issues. It's not something to be done on a regular basis and was done only for instruction purposes. If you've created space, client releases go to ground effortlessly.

Other types of releases include fascia releases that are quite powerful, including unwinding in the fascia. Most energy is in a spiral, and spiraling that out and removing it to reverse the spiral can be powerful. Remember to do it gently, and allow it to go to ground.

CRYSTALS

The three power crystals can enhance the healing session by doing pure chakra work. I have found this very helpful for clients. Place your hands on each chakra, one at a time, and call in the primary crystal for that chakra. This is an allowing with intent, like all the energy field work. If you have your own primary, then calling in the client's for her highest good will work easily. Adding the first crystal to each chakra will align them for relaxation and healthy flow.

TANGENTS IN THE SESSION

If you operate in the mystic realm, past lives, past events, and other cosmic occurrences may arise in a session. Acknowledge them, and be with them for a time. You must assess whether it's your issue or the client's. Before assuming it's the client's stuff and sharing it with him, determine whether it's really yours. If it's his, decide whether it needs to be brought up immediately.

I've worked with many victims of childhood abuse. I can see those events like movies in my head. Yet the client may have blocked the events from her conscious mind. Opening her up to these events must be done gently, if at all. It is important for clients to get it and see it on their own. Some gentle nudges may help. I use probing comments and questions like, "Tell me about your relationship with your father," or "I sense some issues with your mother. What could they be?" Don't push the matter, especially in the first session. If you are not a trained therapist, use common sense, but some understanding of psychology would help here. If you are not comfortable talking, don't worry; the healing energy alone in the affected area will help clients remember when they are ready.

Listen for messages from the patient's guides and angels. Clients may be more attuned to the mystic realm than you are. You can learn from them; they may lead you through the healing and allow you to see more clearly. Go with the clients, and be aware you are just nudging them in the path that leads to their healing.

For example, I've had clients who smoke. I have found that using intuition creates a smoke screen that blocks clients from feeling certain issues. I must honor this habit as a coping mechanism. I never tell them to stop smoking because it helps them cope. Instead, we try to find the root cause of the smoking and heal that. Then, the need for smoking will be removed. I may tell them, "I can spend half my time releasing the toxins from your smoking, or you can stop smoking, and that will make the healing that much more productive." However, I have to honor their smoking because they may very well need smoke around their heart chakra and throat chakra to help block and defend. Everything has to be honored for what it is.

With addictions in general, if it's harmful, work with the client to end it. Cutting back may be a better, attainable goal.

Concluding (with Balance)

I usually end the session at the clients' feet, ensuring they are grounded. At the end, I like to pull my hands away, caress their auras, and do a final balancing above the chakras. Then I step away and close my hands. A small ritual can aid in a balanced conclusion.

When a client leaves, clear your space. Clear the room, and remove all the energies from the client and any of your own issues that arose. Cleanse the table by washing it with energy so it's ready for the next use. Cleansing and creating space between sessions is essential.

Diagnosing

Clients need to know that you have the ability to walk through their bodies. Explain this to people before you do it. Legally, you can't diagnose clients, but if you find something wrong and know what it is, advise the client to see a doctor right away.

Left-Sided and Right-Sided

I want to address left-side and right-side aspects of healing. These are not absolutes, but the left side is generally the maternal side and the right the paternal. Issues with children, mothers, or females will most likely appear on the left side. Issues with vocations (especially if those vocations are male-oriented), fathers, or men in general, most likely appear on the right side. Be aware that left brain/right brain can be opposite to this rule, due mainly to the two superimposed beams—a beam flowing up the right foot, crossing at the thymus, and up the left side of the head, and an opposing one flowing out the left foot.

Also related to this:

- The left-side brain is where we can first perceive a psychic attack.
- Arms are generally linked to work issues.
- Legs have to do with issues about the future.
- Hips are connected to support issues, such as finances, jobs, and career.
- Back problems are tied to the support of the entire structure, career-oriented issues, or deep issues.

MUSIC AND HEALING

Music can open people's hearts; music can heal. Music helps during healing and spiritual sessions, and playing music may help with heart chakra issues. Churches and religious groups use music to open people to accept God's love and energy.

Singing also opens your chakras. Many religions use chanting to open themselves to truth and light. Lower sounds affect lower chakras, and higher notes affect higher chakras. Sound therapy can be used to release many issues. You can try this during an energy healing session. Humming is a good way to work with a client who is unfamiliar with this type of release. Ask the client to hum notes at the frequency that fits the location you are working on, and add the energy to that location to aid the release. The sound vibrations will help loosen blockages.

SELF-HEALING—LISTENING TO YOUR OWN BODY

Your physical body will give you clear messages about health and spiritual and emotional states. It's important to listen to your own body in the same way as you listen to others, but it can be very difficult. Just as doctors should never self-diagnose, and intuitives should not read themselves, it's also hard for *you* to evaluate and heal you. Yet we can call energy into our bodies and work on ourselves.

When you're in pain, work on it yourself, if you wish. Be with the pain, the *dis-ease*. Go into it; go around it. Ask it to leave, if it's ready. Ask it why it's there. Honor it and its reasons for being there. Ask if *you* are the one who should heal it. Remember—you're the sole person responsible for your own health and well-being. If you're to conduct energy healing, you should be well advanced with your own issues, since the energy will bring them up as you work on others. Be prepared by knowing how to release your own blockages.

Be creative in your healing practice. Experiment and try new things. You change with time, and each client requires unique assessment and healing. So enjoy the complexity and vastness of the universe through healing, and don't get hung up on a set method. Paradoxically, it helps to have tried-and-true methods that you can fall back on if all else fails.

Remember *you* are not doing the healing. The energy is flowing from sky energy and earth energy (the One and Mother Earth). It is this divinity that flows through you as a channel to heal. Honor the source of this energy, honor yourself as a channel, and honor the client for the opportunity to heal. You should not be judged if a healing doesn't work. Patients are in charge of their own healing and will only take energy and release as they see fit. You are the facilitator, helper, and bringer of light.

Sing about it, laugh about it, and cry about it, but there are many good reasons for you to be a healer. As a healer, you'll progress by doing and through accumulating knowledge.

CHAPTER 4

THE INTUITIVE SESSION

What is intuition? You think of someone, and that person calls you or texts you, or you meet him or her. You have a feeling something will happen to you or to someone else, and it does. Most people have had similar things happen. There is an intuitive in *you*. An intuitive reading is similar to these small examples but with more focus and intent. You sit with a person, couple, or group and tell them what you sense has happened, is happening, and is going to happen in their lives. We all have this ability.

Intuitive readings are a step beyond basic intuition. Most people can read body language and traits through observation and instincts. A reading allows you to provide names of people and places, times, and actual occurrences that are impossible to see by mere observation or basic intuition. Even so, we all have true intuitive abilities.

(Mind reading isn't possible by people who work with angels and light. I understand that some people practicing in the occult can read minds, but you can easily stop this by using basic self-defense techniques; see chapter 5. Telepathy is one mind talking to another. I believe we, as a race, formerly could communicate this way.)

You must be sensitive to the person's needs. Can this person handle the naked truth? The mind sometimes needs to get things in its own time. Readers must be sensitive, as are healers, not to be destructive with the information revealed to them psychically. You can reveal a truth in a way that allows a person to unravel it slowly, as she can handle it, over days or weeks. This is why many truths are hidden in riddles and parables.

Readings must be for the highest good of the client. Many excellent intuitives won't conduct readings due to their moral code because telling the future (which is only one possible path) is dangerous. These intuitives believe they have no right to read people; clients should get it themselves.

Sessions must be conducted responsibly. An intuitive reading is not about predicting the future or fortune telling. It's about looking at and reading people's energy and seeing where that energy is taking them at that point in time. Then, they can change their energy, their energy field—and change their future. The future is always in motion, and they can choose to change it. If you give people good news, they may change their course for the worse. They may, of course, be able to avoid a rough road ahead. Changing their energy fields by bringing in more divine energy from sky and earth will improve and change their future. Remember not to predict someone's death.

The death card in a tarot deck means transformation; a death of an old way of doing things. The deck I use is by Ellen Connolly. Please see the "Further Reading" section at the back of the book.

There is an issue with conducting intuitive sessions: it is somewhat dangerous. It can be a very positive experience, telling people that they are on the right track and need to keep moving forward. But I'm always concerned about giving people good news and having them sabotage that, instead of going toward the great treasure coming their way.

There's also a flip side if it's bad news. It's nice to see something coming that can be avoided—for instance, a health, financial, or relationship issue could be altered. A good friend came to me often to see if she was heading down the wrong path. I told her about the disaster she was heading for in detail. She changed her direction completely, and then the prediction never manifested. Always make it clear that the clients control their own futures.

INTUITIVE READINGS

You can use many methods to conduct readings: palms, tea leaves, bones, ashes, fire, clouds, and more conventional ways, such as tarot cards. Or you simply read the client. When I do a radio show, for instance, I can make a quick connection to the person, and the details flood out.

People come for an intuitive session for many reasons: problems with relationships, financial matters, careers, or medical concerns. Sometimes it's to connect to past loved ones with their guides. Many people simply want to know where they're heading. There can be deeper, more dramatic reasons that only the subconscious or inner self knows. A good reader asks the client for the reason she has come, and if it's not entirely in line with her inner self, the reader can gently nudge the session toward the truth (or to be more pragmatic, depending on the client's personality).

People often seek an intuitive or psychic reading at a time of crisis. This is the *least* recommended time for a reading. The client's energy is jumping from place to place, dynamic to dynamic, possibility to possibility, and the reading can vary from minute to minute. A counselor must determine if a reading is worthwhile during the crisis or if a healing or other modality is more appropriate. A good intuitive counselor can give a reading at a time of crisis but must give the client provisos and clearly identify the risks. If the client wants a long-term reading, he should relax and calm himself.

Another factor that affects readings is familiarity with the client. Beginners should read friends and family first before practicing on the general public. That said, it's best and most clear to read complete strangers. Readings for family, friends, and even acquaintances will be biased. Foreknowledge and a desire to give only good news will slant the reading. A stranger can arrive in my office and spend an hour while I tell him details of his present and past situations and where he is heading with times, dates, names, and so forth that are all accurate because of the unfamiliarity.

For beginners, it is best to relax through the entire process of learning. I used tarot to start formally reading and tried to use the cards on friends and me at first. This instruction fits with tea leaves or any other type of reading. The tarot (or other modality) focuses your intuition. We all have this ability to some degree, so unwind and allow divine to show you your gifts. Let's start with the tarot deck.

I mentioned my favorite deck, but shop around, use your energy field, and feel the energy through your hands to all the decks you come across. The deck for you will call to you intuitively but will definitely cause a surge of energy out of your hand to the deck (or deck to hand). Purchase the accompanying book for the deck. Take the deck home, and play with it in your hands. Feel the cards flow through your hands and the energy of your hands. Look at the pictures on all the cards without studying them too hard. What do you see in the different cards? Do you see the multiple images on the cards? Look at the design. Ponder the name of the card.

Now open the book that explains the cards and familiarize yourself with the major groupings, the number ascensions, and some of the meanings. Spread the deck out on the table after a good shuffle, pick three random cards, and place them side by side in a row. See how they look together, and then read about each card in the book. Observe the card on the left; does it mean something in your past? Is the center card your present condition? If so, the card on the right is your near future. Memorize, write them down, or snap a picture. Wait a few days, and see if the card was correct. Did the future unfold as the card suggested? Now try it with a friend, just three cards. The friend does the shuffling and mixing up and choosing the cards.

As you get better, try three sets of three cards. Now you have to interpret the cards interaction with each other. This is where a more advanced book can assist you. The book will also suggest other spreads of cards. Remember you are unwinding into your intuition. It is an allowing, a meditating, but as always, it is energizing your energy field. Another trick is if you have your three energy (power) crystals, set them in their natural state, and your intuition will flow more easily. The cards focus you and add confidence to your intuition.

If a friend you are reading is on the phone or computer, just ask him to focus on the cards and ask his questions of the divine while you mix up and pick the cards. After a few readings with friends, you will be amazed how well it works, but if it is not working, try to hold the deck between your hands to energize the cards, or leave the deck overnight with your favorite crystal on top to energize it. I have had a few readings where I've asked the person about her present state, and if the cards did not match, I reshuffled the deck and tried again. Remember to relax into it, and set your energy field. (Also remember to create space, as discussed in the appendix.)

I often use tarot cards because they ground the reading. The cards give me an easy timeline to read. Techniques like these can help you support what you're reading from the person. I like to include a medical intuition in each session. I will also talk with the client's guides and angels, if they want to share with me. Begin a session by reading relationships of people near the client, especially if they're shown in the cards. You may talk for an hour nonstop, giving a lot of information, or you may be interactive, depending on the clients and the situations around them. Clients may be difficult to read, or their inner selves may be blocking. This situation may require a gentle healing or counseling about trust issues, or it could be more complex to unravel. (I've been called the "reader of the unreadable." For me, being creative with a client's blockages aids in breaking through barriers.)

It's best if the client is open to the reading; never force a reading. Often, clients with blockages are unaware of them or why they are there. As a healer, I dwell constantly on the person's well-being. Readers should provide a relaxing setting, put the client at ease, and stress the safety of the process. The client can stop the session whenever she wishes; her safety is paramount. Go through the provisos and concerns with telling the future and the responsibility this holds. Be aware of your client's energy field and your own.

I enjoy radio call-in readings because of the high-paced interaction with people hundreds of miles away and the incredible accuracy and insight that can be attained. For any reading, I strive for truth and genuine perception, encouragement with guidance for self-improvement, and the avoidance of pitfalls. Read in love. A reading can reveal a rocky road ahead, but it often shows that the bumps are required to get the best result.

COUNSELING

Clients may not actively seek self-development, but in my sessions, I feel I have the responsibility to coach and guide them on their processes and paths. My goal is to advance the client in whatever way her inner self requires.

I enjoy encouraging people to a higher level of vibration and dynamic. Developing people's natural abilities in energy awareness, intuition, remote viewing, past-life awareness, and communication with their angels is rewarding. Being a teacher is a great responsibility, as is conducting an intuitive reading. Therefore, make sure you're there for the client's highest good.

I believe each person has an extraordinary unique gift. A reading can open people to the amazing possibilities their gifts hold. If we all could function with our gifts at a higher vibration, our planet and all of humankind would benefit.

I give you now the task of looking up Marianne Williamson's famous quote that begins, "Our deepest fear is not that we are inadequate. Our deepest fear …"

My goal with each session is to reveal the shifts the client can make toward his path, to give possible course alterations, or to affirm the present direction—ultimately, to benefit and educate.

Relationships

Relationships are one of the main reasons people seek an intuitive's counsel, whether it's finding the love of their lives, a parental issue, marital challenges, children, or siblings. The human condition necessitates interaction with others, and it stands to reason this would be a source of struggle. A reading can help a person in creating a healthy environment for a relationship to grow. The main emphasis of a relationship reading is, "Are you ready?"

Unfortunately, relationships are the most difficult aspect to read and have the lowest level of accuracy. This is mainly because at least one other person is involved, and that person is usually not in the session. The reader is being asked to connect and interpret another person's intent without permission. The extent of the reading may be only the effect the other person has on the client and the client's perception. The reading is limited by ethics, if permission is not implicit.

For instance, if I say, "You're going to meet the love of your life at two o'clock on Thursday," this may not happen if the other person changes her mind. If the relationship is new, the attachment or bond may not be strong, and predicting becomes tenuous. I can, though, give a probability. A longer-term closer bond between the individuals increases the accuracy.

In a situation where I clearly don't have permission, such as with former spouses, I'm restricted to reading from a distance and discerning the reactions, energies, and effect that person has on the client. I must honor the other person, thus creating a dilemma.

For relationships such as a child of the client, I probably have permission as long as no abuse is taking place. Child abuse is easy to perceive. I must honor the child. If the child is a teenager or adult, I do require permission. If the bond between them is solid, I can ask the child's inner self easily, and these readings can be accurate. If you read that child abuse is taking place, then your options are limited, unfortunately. You have no hard facts for the police, only intuition. You are best to monitor and observe for physical evidence and then report to police. Police can advise you on your local laws, as these vary from place to place.

Reading people associated with the client, who are in an unquestionably solid, light-giving, reciprocal, and loving relationship, is easier. A loving grandmother, aunt, partner, or other type can be deciphered correctly. The dynamics of relationships make for interesting readings.

You can have great success reading relationships. Just be aware of the challenge. For example, a young lady I'd never met gave me only her first name. I told her she was going to have a poor interaction with her father three days in the future, in the afternoon. She replied, "Yes, I'm meeting my dad at the airport, but in the morning." I told her the flight would be delayed. I gave her insight into why her father was frustrated. This assisted her. Yes, the flight was delayed (that was easier to read than the relationship), and my counsel aided her in defusing the impending argument with her father.

COUPLE READINGS

I enjoy couple readings. Readings with couples or groups bring more dynamics and challenges, but some of the most fun I've had with energy work is when doing readings with two loving people.

Here's an example with a twist:

A couple came in together but wished to be read separately, the woman first. I explained my usual provisos and ethics, and then before laying out the tarot cards, I told her she was having an affair at work and that it was causing her distress. She was shocked and impressed that I knew right away. I suggested she discover just how much this was affecting her and challenged her to live in her truth. I then did a solid, basic tarot reading for her, and we were able to see her best course of action. I promised her I wouldn't tell her boyfriend. I had the discomfort of reading him but was able to give him a factual reading with insight into his career and immediate family. They both left happy. She ended the affair, and these two are now happily together.

CAREER ISSUES

The next most popular type of reading is about careers—finding a job or issues with a current one. Work relationships are easier to read since the personal connection is (usually) much less intimate, and the association is bounded by the parameters of the workplace.

A partnership could be akin to a full relationship-type reading, as this equates to a marriage of sorts. Generally, work-related interactions are less intense, and people's intents are restricted and straightforward enough for a good read. The nonintimate (usually) and nonloving nature of the connections lowers the complexity substantially.

We spend a lot of time at work. Work can be a grounding experience. Primeval issues can arise here, as survival conditions abound. Money to live necessitates, for most people, the need for a job. Blue-collar jobs tend to be at a lower chakra than white-collar work, though someone like a doctor would want all chakras examined for job-related advice.

A bright young woman sat for a reading, mainly to do with her career. I knew immediately that she had two job choices. One was in Calgary, Alberta, and the other was in eastern Ontario. It was very clear that the Calgary position and company was much more positive for her. She was happy that I recommended that choice. It was a fairly easy session to conduct.

Another client had been to four psychics before me, and none of them could read her. I sat with her, but there really was nothing to read, so I asked her if I could send energy to her to discover the blockage. I held both her hands in mine and began a healing-type session, allowing my intuition to flow. In my mind, I asked permission from her to see; then I saw a curtain. It was a heavy black velvet curtain that blocked all light. I told her with my voice what I saw and that she needed to help me draw back the curtain so we could see what was behind it. Sure enough, I asked in my mind for the curtain to draw away, and it moved, revealing light and visions. I was able to read her with tarot and complete a medical intuition that constituted a full reading.

FINANCIAL PROBLEMS

I find pure financial issues clear to read because money is energy and contained—if money is heading toward the client, it's well defined. Unless another person has influence, the theory is sound. If a relationship is involved, then there is higher risk, but a windfall or inheritance is easy to see. We are reading the person's energy regarding the manifestation of a large energy packet, and it will be distinct.

LOTTERY NUMBERS

Many people want to know their winning lottery numbers. I don't conduct that kind of a reading. This is due to the amount of energy and the kind of luck the client must create to win. The client must *decide* to win. I can lead a person through the inner obstacles to winning the lottery. In fact, that's what a reading is all about—the hurdles they need to jump over to get the big win, whether that's a relationship, career, or whatever.

At one time, I personally set out to win a $35 million lottery. I removed all my inner barriers to winning. On my way to purchase the winning ticket, I saw a book on a rack that I just had to pick up. The back cover had a statement that mentioned even the poorest person in Canada is filthy rich compared to most of the world's population. I walked out without a ticket. Someone who lived near me won the lottery.

HEALTH (MEDICAL INTUITION)

I explain to my clients at the beginning of a session that I will hold their hands to scan their health. (It's also a great way to connect with their angels and guides. As a healer, the physical connection aids me with clarity.) This connection allows me to conduct a quick scan of their physical bodies and energy eggs. If it's not serious, I recommend energy healing work and describe the area of concern. Emotional issues can be dealt with in an intuitive reading, but through a body scan, intuitive issues are more pronounced and easily read.

We also can analyze any brain or psychic issues. For example, is the client being psychically attacked or having psychic issues? A problem may come from many areas of the body or just one. If there are issues due to toxins, we could recommend a dietary detox.

Conducting the session from a healing perspective keeps the client's highest good in the counselor's mind. A blend of the medical with tarot and other methods can give an energized reading.

MEDIUMSHIP

Many people wish to connect with deceased loved ones. A woman asked me to help her connect with her dead husband, and this assisted her with closure. If the client is unable to see or speak with the deceased, I know that I am not conducting the session properly, the deceased doesn't want me involved, the spirit is somewhere else, or the client's issues are blocking it. At times, the relationship with the deceased is negative, and the spirit needs to be instructed to leave. The spirit may not be healthy for the client.

MOVING (OR TRAVEL)

Predictions about relocation and travel can be fun. For this type of question, I use the tarot deck. The deck has many travel cards, and the clarity is readily apparent. The tarot gives the relation of the move to other areas (such as work) and gives a date. Once the move card is revealed, details such as location will come to the intuitive.

Using Guides

By guides, I'm referring first to angels, then to saints that the client may have called upon, followed by deceased loved ones and any other light-giving entities. Anything is possible in an intuitive session. Just be aware of the dynamic around the possibility of meeting other beings through the client. I always make sure the angels required for each particular session are present, and I keep the room open so the client's angels and guides can enter easily. Messages from angels (or other guides) are received through the heart and throat chakras, and we talk to them mainly through the third-eye and throat chakras. Open these for clarity.

The Occult

This is interesting work, breaking the bonds of occult-type people and entities. (I use the term *cult* to mean a group of people practicing occult activities.)

The following is one of my personal experiences:

A woman came to me after having three evil cult-type experiences. She was associated with three different groups, and she wouldn't acknowledge the connection until I told her I'd have to end the session. It was an upsetting reading for me, due to her maintained contact with these three dark groups of people and entities.

One of her experiences was with a Malaysian woman who traveled the globe. The second was with a group of cultists in western Canada, and the third was with a voodoo witch living in the Caribbean. After much coaching, she acknowledged that she not only had the contact but was still maintaining it. She complained of a bad back. I told her that this was a symptom of these negative associations. I decided to help rid her of the connections and heal her back.

For all three experiences, she immersed herself in the worship of the dark arts, worshipping demons and practicing dark magic. She gave up her power and allowed these beings in; she allowed the nonlight energy of the cult worshippers inside her energy egg. The Malaysian woman and voodoo witch placed energy blockages that mimicked injuries. The cult group mainly used her energy to channel it into themselves, empowering them to send dark energy and cast spells. This did create energy blockages in her. She was strong enough that the damage done only affected her back. All this was possible because she gave them permission to be in her energy field.

The difficulty with these types of clearings is the attachment. The only way for evil to get inside your energy egg is to be invited in. Once inside, the attachment becomes an addiction. I told her I would psychically break these connections for the next three days. Then she would return for a second session. Over those three days, I worked intensely to free her. She was completely relieved of all her back pain for three days. When I again sat down with her, I explained how she could put up a shield to block the connection to these groups. She practiced with me during the second session. Then, after another three days, I dropped my protection, as I had warned her I would. She returned a week later in great pain because she had dropped her shield. During this third session, I gave her my protection, and the back pain disappeared. Now she was determined to break the contact. Her bad back never returned, and neither did the evil connection with the people and entities.

Past Lives

Past lives often come through in readings and healings. I consider past-life regression to be segregated from an intuitive session. The clients are in control of the healings and readings to a large degree, and their past lives are sacred to them, even if they don't know it.

The theory of past lives is interesting, and many people don't believe in the phenomenon. The idea of traveling with the same group of people or in and out with several groups is part of the theory. Also, we bring issues with us from the many lives we've experienced. Why do children incarnate with leukemia and cancer already in them? Because they're bringing issues from past lives.

Many writers who have studied the original text of the Christian Bible say reincarnation and past lives were once commonly accepted.

Islam has its own teachings. I have found the theory to be real and credible, with many of my own and my clients' experiences to justify it.[3]

I used to conduct separate past-life regression therapy sessions. What I discovered was twofold: (1) the beauty of past-life regression, and (2) the individual can work it out on his own. Clients can discover how to regress on their own.

For a full past-life regression, both you and the person you are doing it for will see the past life. It is very fulfilling work and can help give insight into present circumstances.

Why regress? The main purpose to regress is to heal past issues. What I discovered is that when a life ends, the soul goes to heaven and then decides to come back to this earth, to separate from God, in order to experience and enlighten at this density level. We reincarnate to deal with issues, to develop our souls, and to progress toward enlightenment. Healing past issues can help us break through to why we're repeating—incarnating with certain issues. Past-life issues are not necessarily as significant as issues from this life, but working with them can help with our paths.

The following is a personal story about regression:

A number of years ago, through the course of my own past-life regression, I discovered that my wife from my previous life was still alive in Scotland; she was in her eighties. I decided to try to find her. I was taking business trips to Scotland about once a year, and I knew our names from the past life; in that life, I had been a junior officer in a Scottish regiment. I went to the museum in Aberdeen to look myself up. I told the curator I was a relative and asked her to help me find my "relative" (my past-life wife) and contact her to see if she wanted to hear from me directly. The curator said she'd get back to me.

By the time of the next business trip a few months later, I hadn't heard anything. I went back to the museum on the weekend. The curator was apologetic and confused because her records showed that nothing was sent to me, and this had never happened before. She always answered requests, even with negative responses. She assured me that she would personally look into it and get back to me. I gave her my address again. But I never did get a response.

---

[3] Carol Bowman, *Children's Past Lives: How Past Life Memories Affect Your Child* (New York: Bantam Books, 1997).

First, I had lied, by saying I was related by birth, but I also broke a fundamental universal law—crossing into a past life from a present life. Even the United Kingdom's historical museum system could not break this law of past lives.

CHILDREN

I have three children of my own. Parents have a great responsibility and also a great amount of power over their children. In a healthy, loving, and nurturing relationship, I believe parents have permission to connect intuitively. As my children are now adults, I have verbal consent to heal and connect with them. Children are easy to connect with since they are naturally able to do all of the skills I mention in this book. We are born with full abilities; then they are groomed out.

INSIGHT INTO INTUITIVES

I often hear comments like the following about psychics, intuitives, and mediums: Why aren't they all wealthy? Why aren't they all living the good life? If they're so great at this art, why haven't they won the lottery? Could it be because they are evil?

A doctor should never self-diagnose or self-prescribe because she can't read herself accurately. A doctor is not detached enough to care properly for herself, as she's too involved in the outcome and the issues. It's the same with intuitives. We can't clearly see our own paths. We intuitives also must be careful when reading friends and family because they are too close to us, and we don't want to be harsh. Imagine how this is even more the case with reading oneself.

RADIO AND PHONE READINGS

I enjoy the radio shows I do with Kimmie Rose. Phone readings are incredibly clear because I know only the clients' names and voices. I don't see their reactions. My mind doesn't react to their expressions and start to assume things.

Intuitives must discern and decipher the difference between imagination, intellect, and the intuitive message. Practice all the different aspects of intuition and find what calls to you. Allow your spirit to flow and connect with the energy around you—with the beings who wish to speak to you.

Have fun with readings! As your confidence grows, you will go beyond what I have discussed.

CHAPTER 5

ENERGY SELF-DEFENSE

You can use your energy field to block emotional, spiritual, and physical attacks. Any attack is incorrect, even one that sends love to someone, as gentleness and love can be used to manipulate and hurt as much as anger and hatred. Energy self-defense can keep muggers, thieves, corporations, and demons away—anything with a dark intent.

A workshop is the most effective way to learn the skill of self-energy field control. In a workshop setting, students spar with energy to learn the skills. If you try this without a skilled teacher present, take care, and follow the safety precautions. You will need to be able to set your energy field as described in chapter 1. It is also beneficial (though not required) to be able to perceive your energy egg and core (both the main shaft and the two interwoven beams).

Go ahead and play, but be responsible and safe. These methods for beginners are meant to block energy-type attacks. With basic knowledge as skills, you can readily block energies directed at you.

MY INTRODUCTION TO SELF-DEFENSE

My having a violent youth in this life led me to hard martial arts training to augment my street-brawling skills. I grew up in west-end Burlington, Ontario, Canada, next to east-end Hamilton, a steel town. The gangs in Hamilton killed in broad daylight. One of my best friends was considered too violent for the Hamilton Catholic schools. The Hamilton boys were tough, and they would come for *rumbles*—massive brawls. I'd had naval cadet training and a huge, scrappy older brother. Violence was at home, school, and most public places. I avoided fighting after two separate one-on-one encounters. I resorted to fighting only for protection of loved ones or my life.

I've studied martial arts in most places I've lived, and I always progressed to the point where I could spar. Moving from city to city and starting over with a new dojo and new sensei kept me at a low belt progression but allowed me to learn varied techniques and styles of sparring. I worked with successively higher orders of warrior instruction. My progression in the areas of self-defense coincided with experiences of spiritual attainment and my belief in God. I still have much to learn.

Anyone who has attained a degree of proficiency in a martial art knows that at the highest levels, it develops a spiritual focus and energy defense, the martial art being a mind, spirit, and body discipline. As my spirituality grew, I became aware of angels and energy—different, more enlightened (and nonviolent) forms of self-defense that anyone can do without harm. I shifted away from hard martial arts to energy-defense techniques. From personal experience I can attest that using hard martial arts easily can result in injuries, whereas energy self-defense works to defuse a situation, and no violence takes place.

THE ENERGY SELF-DEFENSE WORKSHOP

Each participant must master the energy-awareness principles before taking this course. Most healing practitioners find the energy-awareness workshop powerful and adequate, and they don't require the self-defense course, which is mainly for personal development.

The sparring that takes place during class requires the utmost energy security or defense field setup. Students will be open to outside influences during the session due to massive shifting and changing of their auras and energy eggs. The instructor must ensure the safety of the students at all times. Every possible eventuality must be considered to secure the site of the workshop. When working without an instructor, each person should create space to ensure safety.

The participants consent to sparring and attacking in a safe environment for self-development and improvement. Coaching is required to show how sparring is used for the higher good of the students. There is a challenge if the class is made up of gentle, healing, holistic people who find the idea of sparring and attacking a fellow student difficult, even if it's for their highest good and for their learning. Energy sparring can be difficult, as it goes against our natural tendency to help, heal, and give aid. Attacking with energy is negative and possibly destructive. Alternatively, if the class is made up of aggressive martial arts students, the class dynamic is a challenge to ensure restraint.

In the harder martial arts, sparring is used to develop the student, showing what it's like to be in actual combat and proving his or her ability for self-defense. However, the instructor makes sure that no one strikes too hard or strikes the wrong areas of the body and that everyone follows basic rules.

That's the essence of the Energy Self-Defense workshop, which takes place in an environment protected from outside energies and entities. Students send energy beams at each other in one-on-one and two-on-one attacks. As the class progresses, they learn more creative attacks. The class understands how the attack feels without defense. Then, when they energize their outer auras, they see how the attacks really have no effect. The outer aura can be ice, mirrors, steel, or light, depending on the attack. Attacks range from hooks, dragons, sludge, sticky jelly, multiple angles, slicing, shifting, and any other possibility. (Higher-level self-defense classes involve deeper skills; conducted in a large wilderness setting, that requires much grounding and preparation.) Experiment with your group, and then utilize these skills in your day-to-day life.

For energy attacks I first strengthen my outer aura with light, and if I perceive the attack interferes with this, I place mirrors all over the outside of my energy egg, pointing outward. For hooks, steel prevents their digging in. If a jelly-or sludge-type of attack makes your outer shell like Teflon, it slides off or brings up energy from the earth in the form of fire to burn it. If an energy dragon is used against you, ask Mother Earth to send a dragon that is larger, or use a diamond outer shield. Your imagination is the best defense in these rare occasions. Power-crystal defense is the most powerful and effective. The only reason to not use crystals is that they may attract unwanted attention from the occult, but with crystals these cult members are powerless. Most of the above-mentioned attacks are those I encounter due to my work against the occult and corporate energies. You will not have encounters such as these often in a normal day.

The auras are all vital to energy self-defense. The main focus is the outer aura, being prudent to stop attacks from penetrating and entering the egg, but the other auras are critical for success. The sixth and second auras are linked to the sacral and third-eye chakras, gaining power directly from the power chakra and the mind. The sixth is at your feet and hands when relaxed, empowering and defending the extremities. The sixth directly supports the seventh. The second aura surrounds the physical body and can stiffen to protect the body, especially if the attack catches you unprepared.

During the street fight in the Yukon when I was a lad (mentioned in the preface), I used all the auras but significantly the fourth or center aura, most affiliated with the heart chakra and unconditional love. At the point when I reached complete love and peace, fear came into my attacker's expression, and he charged at me, bouncing off my egg. Love was the primary defense, and the heart and fourth chakra supported all as a bulwark to attack. To my mind, saying love protected me is uncanny, but my experience that day—and on many since—was clear; love was the full protection.

Enhancing your energy field further is the first aura protecting the vital organs and epicenters of the chakras. Gaining power directly from the energy core is a tough barrier for an energy attack. The third and fifth auras perceive and decipher the attack and create elasticity to the overall defense. These two bend inward and flex as required, adding a different type of strength, much as steel can flex. Energizing these, and all the auras, is required for complete defense. With these two chakras energized, facing fear (solar plexus chakra) and guarding your expression (throat chakra) is the path to peace and harmony required for that perfect self-defense shield.

Aura work will aid you not just in defense but in complete wholeness. These are discussed here in relation to conflict, but all the auras will support a healthy and peaceful life experience. Peace, love, self-respect, forgiveness, hope, and joy can all be enhanced by aura work—as well as chakra, energy core (three beams), and angel work—to find happiness.

BASIC SELF-DEFENSE OF THE ENERGY EGG

We humans stand on two legs, exposing our vital areas, because we naturally have a strong energy egg and outer aura. Animals walk on all fours to protect their internal organs. A human, in her own strength and power, need not fear a 1,300-pound grizzly bear. The bear can see into the energy realm and will avoid an encounter with a strong human. However, as a race we have forgotten our strength. We now have a reduced life span, poorer health, less control, and less personal power.

Our greatest enemies on the planet are, unfortunately, other humans. Learning to defend against a determined foe, especially if that person is energy-aware, is a challenge. Of course, the average person won't contact these types of people often or at all. Even when you become a strong light-worker, you must be aware that evil-intentioned people will see you and perhaps seek you out.

Most attacks are easily stopped cold. For most, the best defense is to bring sky energy down and earth energy up to fill your energy egg and physical body. Ensure that the two energy beams are interwoven and flowing freely—the one down the left leg and the other up the right, crossing at the thymus. Blast out the sacral chakra to the limit of your outer aura, and bring the outer aura in as tightly as required to block any attack. (We can bring the seventh aura as close as one inch from our skin.) If you're doing healing or remote work, create an energy shield around your space and hold your egg at its natural relaxed size. In a relaxed, peaceful, and loving state, you are at your most powerful. Fear can drive your determination; just don't be overwhelmed by fear and anger.

I have used energy self-defense in countless encounters. This is my calling; I do not recommend it for the novice. One of the main services I provide is aiding people who have had occult contact or possession. I also complete clearings for communities where occult have worshipped. This draws much attention to me, so many energy conflicts have and will occur for me. Realize this is a conscious choice I have made and is not for everyone. If you set your energy field, heal, do readings, and live a normal life, you should have few such encounters. If you do, however, these techniques will serve you well.

Imagine any type of defense, and it will occur. Play with making the outer aura into mirrors, steel, ice, solids, liquid, flowing water, crystal, or anything that comes to mind. If all else fails, pray, and Father Sky and Mother Earth will come to your aid. (Refer to the appendix for a summary exercise, Create an Energy Self-Defense Shield.)

People who fear demons and other evil entities need to know the truth—that a strong aura of light, without any effort or gimmick, works effectively on these creatures. The natural law governs the realm in which they operate, and we are so strong in our physical form that they are powerless. They will affect you only if you ask them in and really work to bring them in. Based on my experience battling with cults (and other dark workers), I have found that people who channel demons subvert their natural defense mechanisms, and this takes a lot of effort and intent. As a worker of light, don't fear the dark. These entities are powerless. If a demon becomes a pest, it may be because a human is sending it. Use your angels to chase it off. And remember dark entities can't enter through an injury or traumatic event.

DEFENSE AGAINST THE OCCULT—BATTLE EXPERIENCE

Cultists (those who practice occult magic) can be very good at harboring what I call human psychic energy. They can channel the human energy of a group into a few leaders to super-charge them. However, the power comes only from people and any evil entities that serve with or use the cultists. The power is not from Father Sky or Mother Earth, though they may have stolen a small amount. Therefore, combating them is quite possible for a single individual. Use the techniques described here, and the cult will be powerless over you. Bringing in angels will help, and there are more angels than demons in this world.

I've never been a part of a cult in this life. I've gained my knowledge through perceiving from the outside, looking in while aiding clients. The most powerful cults have members in very senior leadership positions in our society. They can control their members through coercion, blackmail, and their vices. Leaders are adept at channeling the power of the group into themselves as a vessel of every member's human energy by using the psychic dark energy to manipulate, control, or covertly or overtly attack.

I have assisted many people with issues regarding the occult and those who practice the dark arts. In one case, community leaders contacted me because many people were complaining about negative energies. I was able to clear the negative source, and the neighborhood settled down. The basic techniques in this chapter are effective; I use them regularly.

A young couple, past clients of mine, contacted me regarding their upset children and the complaints of their neighbors. I had given them an intuitive reading years earlier, before they started a family, and now they had a baby and a toddler. Both children had been upset for weeks with no explanation—crying, screaming, and acting out. All of their neighbors in this working-class community were discussing how the energy was suddenly bad in the neighborhood. I agreed to help them.

After ensuring my personal energy field was set, I set a field around their house for protection. The couple immediately felt a release of tension, a purer energy. The children, who had been upset a moment before, settled down. I then remote-viewed the area surrounding the house. With my mind's eye, I could see waves of dark energy, thirty feet high, flowing through the community over a few square miles. I followed the waves back to their source, a house a few miles away.

I told the couple all would be well, and they were very grateful. I kept the shield up, protecting their home, while I made plans to go to the source the next day. Using angels as protection, I went to within a few hundred yards of the house, exited my car, and walked the rest of the way. I was sending light at the house the entire time. The people there were causing grief to hundreds of homes and families.

That evening the dark energy was cleansed, and the neighborhood went back to normal. I used my intuition to determine the house was being used intermittently by cultists from a large city two hundred miles away. The cult used remote-viewing-type techniques and was conducting periodic rituals. The clearing I (along with the angels) did that night ensured they didn't return—and have not for the past decade.

DEFENSE IN DIFFERENT LOCALES

When I'm camping in Canada's wilderness, where other people can be more than six miles distant, I create energy shields, as I described earlier. I've also had to defend myself in alleys, as in my street-fighting experiences. The following happened to one of my mentors:

He was in a city in the Far East, walking the back streets. There was a commotion ahead in one long alley that had few side passages. A charging bull appeared, heading right for him! He knew he was powerful enough to stop the bull with his energy. But he thought, *Why should I use all that force? A bolt that strong could stop the bull but perhaps stop its heart as well.* Instead, he sent energy to the ground in front of the bull. The bull slipped again and again until he finally fell to its knees, unharmed. Then, my mentor walked past the bull as it calmly rose to its feet and walked away. Can you imagine the many layers of honor and love that a situation like this entails?

All of this is about having your chakras in balance, with the central chakra energized. Yes, the sacral chakra empowers, but the heart truly wins the victory.

Scanning and Avoidance

Scanning and avoiding is an excellent form of defense that can allow you to escape contact and danger. Scanning is a remote-viewing technique that allows you to see an area around you for hundreds of yards or miles. Then you use avoidance to pick the path and movements to keep from being seen or heard.

I once went snowshoeing in the ancient mountains of northern Canada. As I drove on the logging road heading in, I came upon a timber wolf. He ran ahead and then alongside my vehicle. He was large in his January coat; he was magnificent. When I began breaking trail, I did a scan of the area for wolves and bears. I found wolves a long way off to the south and north, none up a hill to the east, and all was clear to the cliff edge west of my position. I was shoeing to the 350-foot cliff.

It was interesting that I stopped scanning at the cliff edge because when I finally made it to the cliff, I saw another timber wolf walking on the frozen river below. I watched him for a half hour while he hunted up the river. I called to him, but he didn't acknowledge me.

Scanning the area when you're hiking and camping is a good idea. In this example, I ignored the space beyond the cliff, assuming there was no threat, and there wasn't. It was a pleasant surprise to see the wolf. Advance scanning there may have changed my route and spoiled our meeting.

INVISIBILITY

Invisibility is quite possible. Becoming undetectable in all spectrums of light frequency takes great effort and skill, but like everything in this book, you can do it. The simplest way is to fully astral project, leaving none of your essence at your body. But first, be sure your body is safe while you leave. This is an extremely advanced skill, but I wish to show you some of the possibilities of your capability.

I prefer a combination of invisibility and blending with the background. Blending in is usually as effective as invisibility without the effort and risk of projection. You must be in tune with the elements and setting, natural or urban, and become one with the background. Combined with scanning and avoiding, this can effectively make you "disappear." Most people have experienced disappearing at social gatherings. Later, other people swear you weren't there. Important: don't do this while driving, as other drivers may not see you!

STALKING

Stalking can be used as defense since it allows you to close in on an enemy or assailant. In this way, you will obtain a description for police or better ascertain more about an attacker. This does begin to take you down the road of "the best defense is a good offense," so be careful. All stalking techniques are possible, and you can include invisibility or background blending of your energy field. Have fun practicing by playing in parks and wilderness.

POWER (ENERGY) CRYSTALS

As part of higher-level self-defense training, the three power crystals are extremely useful.

Energy defense is highly effective, but use of the three power crystals is superior. The primary crystal is impervious to negative energy, as are the others. The primary covers your trunk and energy core, while the secondary can cover all. The third crystal can push out with enough force to knock attackers, causing them to reel back where they came from. In all the exercises in the appendix, the formula is enhanced using the Mother-based power crystals. The exercise Crystal Defense details using the crystals specifically for conflict.

You're not limited to those methods mentioned above. Crystals are one of many possibilities. Be creative, even in crisis, because your intuition can guide you to the necessary technique for the present attack.

MAINTAINING PROTECTION

Fortunately, we don't have to be aware and empowering our energy eggs at all times to stay protected. Setting your field and strengthening it for the first three weeks after a workshop will ensure that the subconscious mind will maintain the protection. Part of the protection is an alarm; you will be alerted of an attack or an impending assault. Then you can stiffen your defense with steel or mirrors on the outer aura. You will learn to trust your defense mechanisms. Use invisibility to avoid harmful encounters. Be creative, and trust that your mind will tell you when to run, hide, or defend (or attack, if you have absolutely no other option). Your mind will also invent the defense that suits you best, so listen and follow your instincts. Intuition is all about instinct. In an assault, instincts are vital. Let your intuition and light guide you. This can be as simple as not going down a road that feels bad (and so you avoid an accident), to knowing when to run or when to strike with hands or feet. By continually working with your energy field, you will find avoiding happens far more often than heading into trouble.

I was walking in the woods and suddenly stopped in a stand of tall fir. I did not know why I halted and was intent on traveling fast, eager to go, but I stopped, based on instinct, and was unable to move. I had heard nothing and could not hear or see anything. I waited, based only on the instinct that made me halt. Then, with a huff, a massive bull moose moved in front of me from the shadows next to a rock outcropping. I would have walked straight into him. My set energy field and intuition worked with my instinct—that sixth sense—and I averted a collision I would not have won.

We all have the ability to sense beyond our energy field and even beyond our sight. Seeing an assault long before it arrives is a great asset for protection. If an alley feels wrong, don't go down it.

Be in your strength. Many people walk safely on the same streets where others are often mugged. Why is that? The people who walk safely are in their strength, and the muggers feel that power and avoid them. Always fight back if you're physically assaulted—scratch, bite, and scream—and the assailant will want to leave the area. The first seconds of an assault are critical. Remember that a kick to the shins, knees, or groin will loosen a hold on you. But with energy self-defense, physical contact need not occur.

It's best to avoid the encounter entirely, and the next chapter will show you the innate ability you have to do just that.

CHAPTER 6

REMOTE VIEWING, DISTANT HEALING, AND ASTRAL PROJECTION

Remote viewing and astral projection are intuitive abilities that allow the mind's eye to reach out, giving us a bird's-eye view of the surrounding area, allowing us to see the visual and energy realm. Remote viewing involves minimal self-energy leaving your personal energy field and astral projection requires much more of your essence.

We all have performed some theme of these traits. When a loved one is far away, and you can feel him and know what he is doing, it is a projection of sorts. That connection to the other person, no matter how far, is what this chapter is about. The next step is to do it with intent and more clarity. This will allow you to stay closer to loved ones and will also enhance distant healing and intuitive readings and more.

REMOTE VIEWING

Remote viewing is in your mind's eye. It's the image you see inside your brain leaping out from you so you can see the area around you, usually from above and far beyond your vision, until it flies a hundred or a thousand miles or more away. It's like watching a movie or an imagined scene. It's difficult to explain without experiencing it. For me, it's like I'm flying above, and I see it all as clearly as being there in person.

Your mind's eye goes to different places and can see. I see friends at a restaurant, and I'm above them, looking down. Or I may be above the treetops of a forest, scanning the area for miles around. When you're in your mind's eye, you see as well as you do normally and perhaps better and from different angles. You can use it to view the room you're currently occupying, seeing points in the room out of the normal line of sight. Martial artists would call it the *eagle eye*. If you're capable of seeing auras and energies, you can see them more clearly by remote viewing.

Every human being can remote-view. I encourage you to try it because it will raise you to a new level of awareness. I have countless stories of the incredible places I've been. The ability is immeasurable, and you can travel anywhere. When conducting a distant healing, you travel in a psychic form. Healing as well as many light-giving actions can be enhanced by remote viewing and astral projection, including (but not limited to) working with angels. The instructions for remote viewing are below in the section "Practicing Remote Viewing." You can skip there but the following describes the ability for those who are interested in the background.

I'm an engineer by profession, so my analytical side wanted proof. I tested it many times to prove to myself that it was real. Later, I realized my children could do it, that we all can do it.

TESTING THE ACCURACY OF REMOTE VIEWING

We all have the ability to remote-view. We just need training. When I began, I wasn't sure how it worked. Here's what happened:

I was fifteen years old and on maneuvers with the Royal Canadian Sea Cadets in the coastal mountains of British Columbia. The Canadian navy has no marines, so naval personnel must learn land combat and survival. In this training, instructors conducted simulated attacks on us.

One evening, our camp was attacked. Our perimeter held, with losses. On the last day, we suspected an ambush. I was leading a section of ten cadets at the rear of our thirty-man company. We were following a roadside ditch when I called a halt. I could see, in my mind's eye, all the instructors hiding in ambush ahead at a sharp corner in the road, where it dipped between two rocky outcroppings. I warned of the ambush, but the other leaders wouldn't listen. I took half my men on a flanking maneuver, as I refused to proceed into the ambush. I was correct, and I then knew I had a gift.

After that, I began picking up on a lot of energies—auras, angels, and guides—but my analytical side demanded more proof. I required empirical data to prove the phenomena. I did many remote viewings and tested it with friends all over the world. I continued until I trusted the ability. Unfortunately, I also panicked a number of people and realized I needed to use it wisely.

As I remote scan a town or city, I see the energies as shades of gray, from black to white. I see the bright white of a beautiful synagogue, the darkness of a satanist priestess's occult center, the darkness of a corporation, spots of light from godly people, and the many patterns of gray that are our world's various issues and obstacles.

Another story:

I was doing regular hands-on healing treatments with a cancer patient in her home. Her husband was always around when I worked on her, and he was intrigued by my work, as well as by my wild stories of remote viewing. While working with her, I met all four of their daughters. One taught skiing in Alberta; one played cello for a European city orchestra; another taught school in northern Italy; and the last lived in Sydney, Australia.

One time, they asked me to come early to work. The husband welcomed me into their kitchen, where he had set up a tape recorder. He said that his daughters were a part of an experiment he wanted to conduct with me. He wanted me to tell him where all four daughters were and what they were doing. He'd record it and check with them. I told him I needed permission from his daughters, and he guaranteed me they had given their consent.

I then gave him a detailed account of what they each were doing, what they were thinking, and where they were. He had chosen a time when all four were not in their normal locations. The daughter in Alberta was driving in British Columbia, had just broken up with her boyfriend, had dropped CDs on the floor of her car, and was feeling frustrated. I told him in great detail about her feelings, her surroundings, and more. I repeated this for the other three, who were nowhere near their homes.

A few weeks later, I arrived to do more healing work. The husband looked at me as if I had antennas sticking out of my head. He had let his daughters listen to the tape, and my information was completely correct. He was freaked out but still allowed me into his home. The test was conclusive for all of us: remote viewing is real.

DISTANT HEALING

Distant healing is a form of remote viewing. Remote scanning of the body while conducting a hands-on treatment is remote viewing. You can "walk through" a person's body to scan the organs and fascia for irregularities. I most often scan in the energy realm. This helps me see the blockages and issues more clearly. When conducting a healing from afar, I can see the room and the person. In fact, I can't do distant healing without remote viewing.

I learned distant healing during a second-level Reiki course, when my remote-viewing capabilities fully revealed themselves. Here's what happened:

I needed to work with someone who would receive the distant healing. This was a friend who had laid hands on me during my first healing experience. While I was sending him healing during the course, he lay on a table in his home at an agreed-upon time of day.

I then performed distant healing on him during my afternoon class. I was about fifty miles away. When I worked on him, I could see the room and determine details about the contents of the area as if I were there.

The day after the healing, I told him about the room he was in. I even gave him the titles of books on his shelf and where items were placed. I'd never been in his house. He's an analytical person, and he was completely convinced that I'd been in the room, yet he knew I had not. The details of my description convinced me that my experience was real.

This is what happened during my first solo distant healing:

I was asked to heal an acquaintance's baby daughter, just six weeks old. The family lived nearly three thousand miles away. They had taken the baby to several hospitals and doctors in her short life, but she was dying. No one knew why. The father was preparing for a trip to the Far

East to see a healer of some repute. He had heard from a mutual friend that I was into "some kind of spiritual healing," and he asked if I would help heal her. I told him I'd work on his daughter for two weeks, every other night, and that we'd talk again.

I kept my promise. At the end of the two weeks, I called the father. He was ecstatic! His daughter was fully recovered. Many people had been praying, but every night when I worked on her at the appointed time, he and his wife could feel the healing energy and my presence.

After he expressed his happiness, I told him that God had healed her, not me; I was just a channel. I had done astral projection during the healing, and I wanted him to tell me if I was correct in my visioning. While I was working on her, I found that I actually flew though the sky to the space above his house, and then I moved through the front door to his daughter's room. He was silent as I described his house and his daughter's room in detail. I described pictures on the wall and other details of the nursery.

When I was finished, this man, who had been praising me, now yelled at me with intense anger! He accused me of traveling the three thousand miles, driving to his house, and breaking into his home. He told me never to contact him or his family again, and he slammed the phone down.

I was hurt by his accusation, but I was excited too. My remote abilities were true! This was really happening. I could really do this. But there was a dilemma, due to ethics. I had to be more careful. And I began to discover that I wasn't alone. Many others had the same gift. Finally, I realized we *all* have the gift. I began to trust and believe that I had an ability that was real. And we all have that ability.

ASTRAL PROJECTION

Compared to remote viewing, astral projection is more intense. With remote viewing, your eyesight travels, and you can see the details. Astral projection is when a part of your *essence* is present in the remote location. You see as with remote viewing, but parts of your energy field and soul are there as well.

There are different degrees of astral projection. The people at the receiving end will feel you more readily. Be aware that the more of your essence and soul that goes to the location and resides there, the more dangerous it can be for you. Know how to protect yourself before attempting a projection, and begin small, allowing only tiny parts of you to go at the beginning. When you are more practiced at self-defense, try sending more of you (if you wish).

With healing, I find that astral projection gives a clear and powerful experience for the client, with the associated increased potential to aid. Other reasons are linked more to my work in service to Mother Earth and the High Lord.

An example of astral projection:

A beautiful Czech couple came to me for insight, and I gave them a structured reading. I thought I wouldn't see them again for some time, but they returned a few days later with an interesting request. They wanted me to connect them with the woman's recently deceased mother, which I did. They spoke directly to her. They were very satisfied with the session. I didn't expect to see them again soon, but the next day they were back again. Now, they wished to astral project to Prague. Her mother's spirit was back home. There was a wake for her in the city near their hometown, and they wished to go there.

As I trained them, we joined hands—the physical link securing our connection to each other—so I could then lead them in astral projecting. Within a half hour, they were doing it on their own, as I just observed them and ensured their safety. When we began our trip, we all sat holding hands.

They each followed slowly as we flew out above Ontario and then over Quebec, moving much faster. The acceleration increased until we were above the center, where the wake was being held. We hovered above a unique building in Prague. They told me that this was the location of the wake. The building was round, much of it glass. I stayed above, and they went inside. After a short while, the man came back outside to tell me that everybody was there. He had seen his family, his own mother, all of them. He could see everything that was occurring and was later able to call his family and verify the dancing and other detailed events.

There's no question that we were in Prague. (I've never been to Eastern Europe.) When we returned, they were both in tears and so happy that they were able to attend the wake. It was a first experience for both of them. They can now astral-project on their own without my aid, and they're now more connected to their families.

As you move along the path of light, you will naturally gain these abilities. We all have this gift, so play with it. Have fun and learn.

PRACTICING REMOTE VIEWING

Before conducting a remote view and certainly before astral projecting, you must master the skill of Create Space and Create an Energy or Crystal Self-Defense Shield (refer to the appendix). Make your outer aura and space safe, and ensure that the energy around your place is solid and strong. Spend time concentrating on that shield and your strong outer aura. If you don't believe you're in a place of strength, wait for another time to begin. Call in angels as added protection. Clear your energy fields as much as possible.

Once your safe space is created, relax and imagine a bird—any kind of bird—sitting on your shoulder. This imagined bird will be the vehicle for your viewing, the focus of your energy and mind. Focus on this bird and imagine it as real. Relax, breathe, and look through the eyes of the bird. Once you can see through its eyes, then allow the bird to fly around the room and perch wherever you wish. Do this a few times until you feel in control of the bird. This energy bird is a part of you in bird-energy form. Now, let the bird fly out of your space. Fly out over the area around the building you are in and view the landscape. You can also scan the area for energies, to see the different energy fields created by people and nature. Open your mind to all possibilities.

Bring the bird back close to your space, and ask if it was followed. If the answer is yes, ask your angels to chase away the energy. If it is human energy, you may need to push it back to where it came from and then return to your safe space. As you do this, watch for undesirable humans who may track your movements. If your space is secure, you need not fear. As a light-worker, you will be safe. When your bird is safely back, relax, breathe, and end the session. A clap of your hands will do nicely.

You can then physically walk or drive around your area to discover if what you saw in your remote view was accurate. Did you see a community event at a park in your viewing and was it actually there?

You could set up with a friend to be outside, doing an action unknown to you, remote-view it, and then call and describe what she was doing. When I was first learning, I'd find an event or out-of-the-ordinary sight and then later walk or drive there to verify the accuracy. This helps build confidence.

After about five scans of the area around your space, venture further afield. Start moving the bird faster, and you may begin to view without the bird. If I ever struggle to view, however, I come back to using my energy-bird, and it works every time.

To make it easier, another person can work with you. Be sure you're protected. The protective shield can be with both of your energy fields. You can verify what you see when you leave your space with your partner. In that way, you'll qualify your experience (but it's not necessary). With another person, you'll be able to tell the difference between imagining and actual viewing. The best way to discern is to experiment.

There's a lot of responsibility attached to the ability to see and travel anywhere. You could watch somebody type a password into a computer. You might sense that someone has been injured but doesn't want anybody around. You can walk into people's apartments. The code of ethics for normal physical interaction doesn't encompass remote viewers, given their ability to see through, feel, and perceive people much more deeply than looking at them with normal vision. I believe people who are given this ability (and it is possible for all) also are given a high moral sense. Remote viewers are challenged because there are no remote-viewer police.

As a remote viewer, I've been tested on many occasions. I can go anywhere at any time. I've amazed and freaked out so many people that I hardly do it anymore. For me, to hurt or bother someone with this ability shuts down my ability to remote-view. I have built-in ethics. My body hurts if I use the power even slightly wrong. When you view, keep your moral compass strong.

In a way, we are very connected through the Internet, but what about using remote viewing and astral projection to connect with faraway tribes or even angels? Imagine a world where we could all be connected like this! I believe it would improve our collective consciousness to have this enlightened connection with all humankind. A modality such as crystalline conscience technique is an example of our attempt to connect energetically as one human race.

The following is a good example of a code of ethics:
Remote viewing shall

- always be for the highest good of all people involved;
- be conducted only with incontrovertible permission;
- be used only for healing, defense, and self-defense of children or loved ones; and
- ask for the guidance of angels before, during, and after use.

FURTHER THOUGHT—TELEPATHY

Yes, it is possible to have telepathic communication between humans. Based on the many past-life regressions I have done with individuals, I have discovered that millennia ago, we were capable of this form of communication, and we're moving back toward reclaiming this ability. Many people feel intuitively connected to others who are close to them, but I have met people—strangers—who have known what I'm thinking. Women are perhaps more adept at it. I have experimented, and it works.

An intuitive reading is the beginning of telepathic communication, but I'm referring to actual thought-to-thought communication. Presently, this is a rare occurrence among humans. Now and then, I telepathically communicate with a saint of a lady who lives northwest of Beijing. She is a remote viewer, and her granddaughter has the gift as well. They are busy ladies working to improve the lives of countless children, but we always have time for good conversation.

CHAPTER 7

ANGELS AND OTHER BEINGS OF THE MYSTIC REALM

There is a battle going on. I've seen it. Is it for balance between light and nonlight? Is it good versus evil? I only know that I follow the light and try to be a servant of the One, who has will and no ego.

Most of my work and effort is done with the aid of angels, and angels are for light. Angels sing, heal, guide, protect, and sometimes fight. I want to share a bit of the vast knowledge base of these most magnificent spiritual beings. Then we'll branch out to lesser beings.

ANGELS, OUR GUIDES

Angels are some of the most powerful spirit entities in the mystic realm. I see them as the Christian Bible describes them. They are not omnipotent, but they are extremely powerful. They honor us and our power. They guide, protect, teach, comfort, and speak to us.

Angels can guide your path and will come to you when required, even when you lose your awareness or focus or when you sleep. They travel faster than light and have many varied abilities. All their accomplishments, traits, and skills would fill volumes, but here are some basic characteristics of angels:

- Angels are well organized and lawful.

- They fight and protect.
- They heal and nurture.
- They bring light, holiness, fire, and truth.
- They are messengers.
- They have mirth, music, love, and joy.

These are a few of the characteristics of angels. There is a clear command structure, but this is a hierarchy that works without prejudice and with all honor. For example, you may find the archangel Michael listening and learning from the lowest angel of the order because they operate without ego. These are the archangels' attributes, in brief:

Michael: healing, insight, protection; blue light, throat chakra

Gabriel: warrior, protection; green light, heart chakra

Ariel: guidance, inciter; indigo light, third-eye chakra

Zekiel: truth, strength; yellow light, solar plexus chakra

Edrial (or Jophiel): love (power), rejuvenation, illumination; orange light, sacral chakra

Raphael (or Uriel): wisdom (truth), connection/communion to the One; violet light, crown chakra

Nadrial: nurturing, all-consuming fire; red light, root chakra

COMMUNICATING WITH ANGELS

Opening the heart, throat, and third-eye chakras will help you see, hear, and speak to angels. They can become visible, but they seldom do. Many people who struggle for good claim to have seen angels with their own eyes. We have pledged to become a part of this physical existence, whereas they have not. They are for the heavenly, spirit realm—the mystical realm.

To see them, first begin with hearing them. You don't have to do anything more than work with your energy, cleanse your body (dietary detox), and clear your energy fields.

Learn to scan and be at one with nature, slowing as you grow in awareness. Then, you'll begin to hear the angels speak to you. Talk to them; ask them to move or to help you. Just know that they hear you. Then ask to see them. Ask others to come and watch as more angels come in. It's a great advantage to work with other people who can see angels for verification.

Gender for angels seems to be a manifestation of their character and hidden nature. This is the connection between gender and chakras: crown, throat, heart, and solar plexus chakras—male; third-eye, sacral, and root chakras—female. Others may perceive them differently, but angels are complex creatures and will appear to you as you require.

When I am in a room with another person who can see angels, we both pick one angel to observe and describe. The results are surprising. We see the same creature, general shape, color, and size. The name of the angel may be the same or completely different. It will speak, and we will hear it in our preferred language, but many aspects will differ. My partner may say the angel is a healer with a profound message to all humankind, and I may see the angel as a protector in armor, with a sword and shield ready to protect us. Yet for all our awareness and intuition, there is much more going on with this angel, no matter the circumstances.

Angels operate in a different realm and have intuitive and physical abilities far beyond ours. They can remote-view effortlessly and multitask, allowing them to see in hundreds of places at once while processing this data and determining their course of action—all while sending healing energy, fighting a battle, sending a message of guidance, and comforting someone at the same time.

Each one has a multitude of abilities and a unique character. They appear displaying the traits that you require at that particular point in time. The same angel may work with you or come to you on several occasions and seem like a different one each time. All angels have the basic traits mentioned above and are imbued with much power from the One (God) and therefore can function in limitless capacities. Angels are there to aid you. Call on them in all situations.

From a self-defense perspective, angels will come when called. Realize they also leave immediately if you ask them to leave. This is the same for demons and other mystical entities. Your will and energy field overpowers them. (The only reason for a demon to be around you is if you called it or it was sent. If it was sent, blast it with energy, and it will run. This is an occasion when attack is justified. Demons exist only for negative reasons and are for a much lower good than your highest good.)

ANGEL EXPERIENCES

If you need an angel's presence, just ask. The angel will be with you in less than a blink of an eye. Call on them for any reason. Angels aid in healing sessions, prayer, joyful occasions, rituals, and all aspects of life.

The following story shows the power of angels:

One day I was running through ancient woods, heading to a dojo, where I was training. I was speaking with the trees, as I often do in the woodlands, when I suddenly stopped. Just under the surface was a host of angels. They asked if I wanted to be a part of a battle against a cult. All the saintly people in the town had been praying, and this was the answer. The angels attacked and destroyed the cult, removing the taint from that town. The battle flowed into another city that housed the higher-level cell. The cult (its dark energy, entities, and demons) was expunged. The human members left, bereft of power.

The experience was bizarre. I astral projected, flying with the angelic host. The balance of light and dark was restored, in answer to prayer. It was exhilarating! Afterward, remembering I had been called to the dojo, I continued my run.

Once there, a higher-belt-level student told me that only brown and black belts were allowed in. The sensei came out and personally invited me back in. His energy-awareness skills were such that he knew that my true level of self-defense was much higher than my midlevel belt progression. I stood with him to watch the class, which an instructor from Japan was teaching. He was a master of masters and spoke no English. He felt my energy, and I felt his, and I knew that I was connecting with a fellow warrior from a past life. I bowed, and he returned it. He studied me for a moment and then broke out in a knowing grin. I knew (based on my intuition) that he sensed that I had just been in the angelic battle, a battle he was aware of and perhaps a part of. We spoke no words to each other, both knowing that the connection was enough and complete, a telepathic communication. The instructor-warrior had called me to the dojo so that I would go through the woods and meet the angels. I moved from the town shortly afterward, and I've continued this work for other communities.

Years later, I had another incident where angels saved me. I was running on a trail, up and down cliff escarpments. The trail was familiar and clear, with dusk settling in. Suddenly, I tripped on a log and fell flat. An angel yelled, "Stay down!" I obeyed, and there was a blast of earth and brush twenty-five feet to my right, east of my position. A blast of energy had been sent by a cult world leader far to the west. The angels had tripped me and saved me from injury. This gave me an opportunity to deal with this powerful dark leader.

Many other people have angel stories that are far better than mine. Believe that angels are there, real, and able to assist you. Don't ever fear the occult. The High Lord rules all.

A note regarding saints—people who have died after living a godly life on earth. They aren't angels or ghosts, but they can help. I've asked them for guidance, and I find great comfort and wisdom in speaking with saints. Their understanding of the human experience makes them excellent counselors.

A final note involves the archangel Ariel and Kimmie. In the foreword, Kimmie mentioned our first meeting. This took place at an event with many people, though Kimmie and I had some time together just beforehand. That was when her account took place. When driving to the event I had asked (or called) for protection, and Ariel came. I asked Ariel to leave, since an archangel would have better things to do. I suggested one of her followers, but Ariel ignored me. When Kimmie and I met, Kimmie heard Ariel. She asked me why she kept hearing Ariel's name, so I told her the story. Afterward, as the event was breaking up, a woman stopped me and asked why a whole host of angels was with me. I had no answer she would believe, but it was Ariel's doing. Yes, angels are real, and yes, you too can see and converse with them.

SPRITES AND FAIRIES

These joyful, playful, and loving creatures are another miracle of God's creation. I often see sprites and fairies in my travels. My work is more with angels, but I'm glad a fair lady led me to see joy rather than always war.

I was in the midst of one of the innumerable spiritual wars when I was honored to meet a fabulous group of people at a social gathering, all light-workers. A beautiful woman acknowledged my angelic mission but sweetly asked if I'd ever noticed the lesser mystical creatures, such as sprites and fairies. Her stories challenged and intrigued me. The stories were varied and light in nature and didn't really sink into my memory, as my work is mainly angelic. Each time she spoke, however, I was taken to a magical, wondrous, and joyful place and state of mind. I was left with a longing to explore these creatures more. I asked the angels, Mother Earth, and Father Sky (High Lord) to show me these creatures and teach me about them.

Soon after, I was blessed with a business trip to Scotland, a glorious land. I was free on the weekends to hike and travel. Walking in the Grampian Mountains, I came upon a babbling brook set in a green wooded hillside. Where the water rushed over a rocky outcropping to fall a few feet into a pool, I saw the sprites. They were filled with joy and mirth as they frolicked in the release of energy from the turbulent waters. I was awestruck and enthralled, yet my eye was drawn upward. There, I gazed into the greenery of the ancient wooded ceiling to see fairies playing among the tree foliage.

Being in tune with the environment is key to seeing these and all mystical creatures. In a relaxed, clear state, they will come to you and bring messages. In chapter 1, we discovered that the heart, throat, and third-eye chakra and thymus gland are key areas of angelic connection. By opening up and energizing these areas, you will see, hear, and speak to angels. I had major throat and thymus issues in my twenties and thirties (always getting the flu and sore throats). Once healed, I was able to connect to the angelic realm. Focusing on the two opposing energy beams that cross at the thymus will aid greatly in angel work.

Since these beams are closely linked to the thymus, they are significant in working with angels. Seeing and speaking with angels is greatly aided by energizing these two streams of energy. Messages generally flow down the left side of the head, and speaking flows up the right-side beam. To hear the angels, ensure the beams are flowing well and cross at the thymus. Imagine their voices coming down the left side of your head (against the flow of energy) and flowing up, as you speak, the beam on the right side of your head, opposing the flow. You may find the thymus aches a bit, so have one hand over it while speaking and listening. Talking with angels and receiving their messages charges the thymus, aiding your immune system, bringing better health. I recommend doing it throughout your day, every day. Angels are there to aid you.

Today, I am learning more and have much more to learn. For me, these creatures return me to joy that I have always struggled to find. Not long ago, I discovered a hidden waterfall, untouched by humans, and when I stand by the waters at its base, I can't control my laughter. Hundreds of sprites frequent that place. I've returned there since with the same experience, to stand at the pool's edge with mist all around, filled with mirth and joy.

I don't claim to know much of angels, and I know even less of all these creatures. Explore the mystic realm as you wish!

GHOSTS AND POLTERGEISTS

Another amazing person I met at that special gathering was a man who worked with energy, and he clearly read my energy field. He taught yoga, among other things, but he loved ghost work. With a group, he'd spend evenings at cemeteries, causing large numbers of ghosts to emancipate—to be liberated, allowing them to leave and go to heaven.

He explained that ghosts are the souls of people whose bodies have died but their souls are trapped here, commonly due to unresolved issues. They cannot or will not go on to heaven, and therefore can't reincarnate.

These are human souls who refuse to deal with their stuff, and they don't want to shift. Ghosts hang on to anger, fear, or desire and are unable or unwilling to release the past, so they stay. Perhaps they hope a loved one will return to them, and so they remain in the spirit world—lost, not realizing the futility of their existence. This new friend travels to locations that harbor ghosts, gently instructs them on their plights, and then nudges them to heaven.

It's quite a task to which he is called. I commonly come across souls like this, and they run from me, knowing that as a healer, I will release their pain and allow them into transition. Some do want release and will allow me near. My friend does not force them to go and treats them with kindness; they do have a longing to release and leave, yet issues hold them here. Being individuals, it is unfair to generalize about them, and each ghost or entity deserves dignity and respect. Once, while dining with friends at a restaurant in an old house, I realized a ghost was there. Everyone took turns going up into the music room of this old house, trying to find her. I distantly connected with the ghost while I was having my dinner, and she asked me not to look for her because she knew that this would start to release her issues and bring comfort, forcing her to confront those issues. I respected her wish and refused the owner's invitation to go upstairs.

I've had many spiritual experiences with ghosts, such as the following:

One day I met a client whose son was having negative experiences that were ghost-related. Mystical creatures were appearing to him as monsters, and items in his room were scattering or rattling. Disturbing energies were directed at him, causing nightmares. This client was trying to sell her beautiful century-old home, and she felt that the trouble her son was having was related to the lack of potential buyers. I told her that her son was correct—entities were around and in her home.

On a dark December evening, I visited her. Her husband was also a client, and I met their second son. After a quick scan of the property, I understood the matter. My scan was a remote view and intuition (mediumship), one that revealed information about a servant girl who had lived on the property. The ghost of this young woman quite openly told me her history, what had happened to her, and—most important— why she haunted the place. There had been a coach house at the back of the property before World War I, with maid's quarters in a loft above the main floor. The owners of the house had horribly abused the maid, including sexually assaulting her in public. She finally killed herself to end the suffering. She was now haunting the back corner of the property, which included the part of the house near the son's room. Over the years, more ghosts had joined her haunting, and now dark entities were showing up. These nonghost entities were bothering their son.

To honor the deceased young woman, I asked the current owners to allow women to aid me. The women were friends of the owners. I intuitively described women I saw in their circle of friends whom I sensed had intuition, who would be open to aiding, and with whom I could work. Since the servant girl had been assaulted mainly by men (though not exclusively), I felt she would be more amicable to the feminine energy. Also, given the extent of the corruption on the property, having more people would provide beneficial support, prayer, and empowerment. The four ladies and the owner all added to my knowledge of the history and to the situation. Their sense of the maid's feelings also created a place of wholeness. I sensed that the additional feminine energy would allow for a quick and complete clearing of the property and release of this tortured soul.

With the four women present, we gently explained to the maid-ghost that her presence was disturbing a child. It wasn't her but the other entities who resided on the property, due to the negative energy from what had happened to her. That negative energy didn't come from the ghost, but from the disgusting abuse she had suffered. I could not release the negative issues without affecting her. She had to go, along with all the vulgar energies.

We honored her. We acknowledged how wrong the abuse had been. We asked if it was time for her to transcend and move on. We also showed her that because of her haunting, a child had been frightened. Some of the ghosts who had joined her on the property did not have the best intent, and we explained just what her act had done. Throughout all of this, she wept. She felt compassion and sorrow for the situation.

For most of the clearing, the servant girl hovered above the darker energies and other ghosts, looking down with sad eyes. She stood at the place where she once had been on a platform while barbarity was committed against her. She looked with sad eyes at me and the women assisting. Intuitively, I felt her sadness for her loss and sadness that she had frightened a child and brought harm to the property. We told her it was okay and not her fault, but if blame should be placed, it would fall on her abusers and their heinous actions. She smiled at the end as the women sent her love, and she released the guilt, shame, and hurt—or so I imagined, based on her angelic gaze. Then her ghost fell into the earth, and Mother Earth received her. Her spirit was free. Those with me and I felt that shift and the love that followed. All of us were honored to have been a part of the healing.

She allowed us to heal her. We worked on her remotely with distant healing techniques, and then she was ready to depart. She apologized to the boy's mother by speaking in my mind. When she left, she took with her a number of ghosts and an energy structure that she had kept around this public event. All of this energy went into the earth, and Mother Earth took it back. After she departed, we were able to clear the rest of the house and the property, which sold a few days later. These types of clearings are usually less involved, but the haunting parties should always be respected.

Poltergeists are a natural phenomenon and are not to be feared. A spirit or a ghost can be in control. If it is bothering you, ask it to leave, or clear it as you would a ghost. Also, energy self-defense tools will work.

As an additional note, sometimes loved ones come to people and just hang out for a while. These spirits are common and are not necessarily ghosts. For three or more days, the spirit of a person may stay and visit loved ones before transcending to heaven. These spirits can be helpful—or menacing. Like ghosts, they are easy to send away if you wish, but they may not always come when you want them to. Basic self-defense is very effective with these phenomena, if required.

CHANNELING

I define channeling as allowing a separate, willful spirit to enter your being. The spirit entity fills the core or the energy field inside the first aura and, therefore, most of the physical body volume. I've done this only with angels; those practicing the occult do this with demons.

There are rewards for doing this with angels. I've done it for the experience. I've done it to heal and release. I've done it for the amazing connection and the pure holiness, joy, and love that angels possess. I ask the angel for permission, which is not always given. You must know the angel's name, and permission must be freely given.

Channeling can be dangerous because you open your seven auras, allowing the incursion. This is an instance when negative energies could easily enter your core through the opening you create. Therefore, this should not be attempted until after the exercises Create Space and the Create an Energy or Crystal Self-Defense Shield are well developed. So before performing a channeling, set up your energy field inside a safe space. I always do this alone to ensure purity and safety. (Refer to the appendix for this exercise.)

Channeling should be done only on rare occasions. This is ensured somewhat, since angels will refuse if you're not ready for the session. I like to combine channeling with a dietary detox so my body and fields are more prepared, and I have a clearer experience.

DEMONS AND EXORCISMS

Humans can channel demons and allow them to take possession of them. This is done by people practicing the occult. The reasons for associating with these groups are many and varied. They are led by the false argument that channeling in this fashion will give them power and abilities. They do gain some additional traits but the cost of being controlled by these vile creatures far outweighs any gains. The process is different from channeling angels. Rituals, sacrifices, and/or other ceremonies are generally performed, with an oath given to never expel the demon. This is why it can be very difficult to exorcise demons. The largest impediment to releasing demons is the person's attachment and will to keep them.

Exorcisms must be conducted with many angels present, with a human commanding them. A light-worker can conduct an exorcism, since the demons are powerless over the worker. If the demons are in the host person by ritual and will, the light-worker must deal with the person first. It must always be for the person's good, with permission and integrity. Ceremony and ritual can aid in the exorcism process, but it's not necessary. Blind adherence to ritual may not be in the best interest of the host person, since ritual and ceremonies may have been a large part of the possession process.

If you're present when an exorcism is being performed, exercise caution and safety. For the light-worker, intuitive insight into why the person allied with the demons is usually necessary. Healing the root cause is vital. Safety is critical after the demons are expelled. Be careful of your boundaries if doing work like this with a possessed party. Have outside support so there are witnesses to what takes place. There is the potential for legal action against you if the situation becomes volatile.

Your best intentions could backfire, so use common sense and law enforcement officers or social workers, if required.

I've had the opportunity to learn more through many similar interactions. Cults differ subtly from one to another but follow the principle of channeling human energy into one or a few leaders. They usually meet on Monday nights, as most religious leaders take a break on Mondays after the holy services of the weekend. A Monday with a full moon is coveted, and they enjoy Friday the thirteenth and all the traditional ritualistic possibilities.

Members of the cults work hard—harder than many followers of the light. I recently encountered someone who was up as early as three thirty in the morning to perform his dark arts. That level of effort can make for a challenge, but with a little diligence, it is easily overcome—the power a light-worker can convey is much stronger than the energy of an entire cult.

Another experience:

A teenage girl whom my wife and I both knew once asked me for help. Her intuition led her to me, and she knew I had the ability to help. I suspect one of her angels led her. She and a group of her friends were secretly part of a cult that believed they were vampires, and they practiced occult magic. She had been lured into the cult by the powers using dark psychic abilities. This developed a bond, a deep hold. The young woman's desire to be in the group and play with the darkness of the energy and power, coupled with a sense of belonging, created a hold on her. It was difficult to break the bonds.

Her parents were unaware of this, and she didn't want me to tell them. Although she was nearly eighteen, I had to be clear about my ethical standards, but I promised not to contact her parents unless she was in real danger. As I mentioned above with exorcism, one must approach this with high integrity and be mindful of possible liabilities.

For the first three days, I worked specifically on separating her from the cult. I put a shield of protection around her. I did my own remote view of the cult so I could locate the source of their energy. I sensed that the cult members were leaders in government, police, or had positions in large and small corporations. I discovered where they worshiped. This was a cell—in fact, a subcell of a cult cell—located in a larger city twenty-five miles away. My scan was accurate down to the exact house. I was able to prove the accuracy of the scan by verifying the location and the connections with the young woman.

The scan showed a slowly sweeping spiral of dark energy centered on the cultists' house. The energy was impacting most of the city. I set up protection for my home and the young woman's.

The cult began to sense me and my scanning. I was new to this kind of work and had much to learn. They began to send beams of negative energy and energy blasts at the energy field I'd set to protect my home, my family, and the field around the young woman. One night, the cult tried to attack my three-year-old daughter with energy. This prompted me to attack back with my own energy. But this was what they *wanted*. By provoking me to attack, I was now vulnerable, due to its dark nature and the fact that now they were involved with me and I with them. I was no longer ignoring them, and they had a hold on me.

In the aggression, I then became dark. Later, I experienced how to attack using the light together with other light forces and how to clear dark energy from people's homes and areas. For now, my attack in anger had created a rift in the shield around the house and had upset my children. I stopped my desire to attack them, and when I drew up the defense, they lost their hold on me and the household settled down.

Over those three days, I taught this girl how to protect herself. She was a fast learner, and at the end of the three days, I removed my shield, and she put up her own. She saw how she could easily block the negative energies. She just needed to keep this up until they lost interest. Eventually, I taught her self-defense, and she successfully broke away from the cult. She praised me for getting her away, but she was the one who broke the ties. During this time, I also prayed, and then I began to see angels around the house, protecting my family. Eventually, the cult itself was overcome with light and angels.

Any work against the occult should be done with angelic aid. They are very willing to oblige. Angels were a part of that young woman's rescue. As I've mentioned, ask and they will be with you in less than a blink of an eye. Call on them for any reason. Angels aid in healing sessions, prayer, joyful occasions, rituals, and all aspects of life.

I've touched on a few creatures of the mystic realms. Trust your angelic guides with anything else you want to learn. Remember that most dark or evil entities work with fear, so a high morale is important. Courage is paramount if you deal in this realm.

No one can damage your soul. Playing with demons will not hurt your soul, but the things you do while possessed are still your responsibility and karma. Angels are there to guide us. Demons are powerless over us; they only gain power if we allow them to. We can use the dark energy. I recommend only light-work and angel-work.

I don't claim to have all the answers and all the knowledge. That is only for the One (God). I try to humbly serve the One with my abilities. The High Lord has given me gifts that I use for light. I wish to help people attain their highest level of awareness. I strive for a higher level of integrity and courage.

There are many more angels than demons. Movies would have us believe that evil is much more powerful than good, but the Bible alludes to only a third of the angels falling when Lucifer turned to evil. Light and good will prevail. What a world this would be if our leaders were able to and actively sought to communicate with the One and angels!

CHAPTER 8

NATURE, EARTH, AND THE UNIVERSE

All living things have a strong energy field—plants, trees, insects, birds, animals, and sea life. The list of creatures on this great planet is almost endless. A remote viewer or distant healer can see these energy fields and the connections between the creatures and flora. It's an amazing miracle of creation.

As your sensitivity is turned up, you can discern even the energy of rocks, sand, mud, and water. These too are connected in the great web of life-giving energy. Mother Earth's energy connects all and provides energy nutrients for our continued existence and enlightenment.

The sun, moon, and planets in our solar system, together with more distant astral bodies, and our placement in the galaxy and universe are a part of the complex web—a web of energy woven for the benefit of all. Tapping into these sources of light and life-giving power will aid you.

Always remember that our primary sources of life are Mother Earth into our root chakras and Father Sky (High Lord) into our crown chakras.

ANIMALS AND BIRDS

As a child, I was interested in animals and birds, and I often walked in the woods to find them. Later in life, I began to study them more. I do enjoy the wilderness. I reference *Animal Speak* by Ted Andrews and the Audubon Society's *Field Guide's to Birds and Trees* quite often. I may be an amateur in tracking and observing, but I feel the life forces and get messages from these wonderful beings. Discovering your own animal and bird totems is excellent fun. Like the Native culture, all races have roots to a hunter/gatherer culture.

All animals have the seven chakras, and certain chakras are stronger than others. For instance, the sacral chakra on a lion is very powerful compared to other chakras, yet all are there and strong. I have experimented with these phenomena in the wilderness often. I have had the privilege to connect with many animals and have found that animals also see energies; they see clearly in the energy realm. When I bring angels in the room, my cat sees them.

We've lost much from losing touch with animals. My animal and bird totems have given me great insight. Many of them sacrificed themselves to me (mainly through car collisions) so I could find their messages. I try to hear Mother Earth's messages to me through animals, birds, rocks, and trees. I'm not always the best listener. Animals, birds, and all of nature will give you your message. Grasp the message of your totem, and add adventure to your life.

I had a few experiences with animals before learning anything about totems. These included grizzly bears, wolverines, and caribou in the Yukon; black bears and moose in Algonquin Park; and foxes and deer along the Niagara Escarpment. There is such richness on this vast planet we call Earth.

From those experiences, I learned a lot about our power over animals. Here's an example:

One summer, I was sent by the army to teach canoeing and sailing in the Yukon. Our camp had been poorly chosen, and I was concerned. On the second day there, a Native boy rode into the camp. When I told him I thought we were in a very poor location, he agreed and invited me to visit his grandmother.

They lived in a trapper's home, actually a converted covered wagon. Grandmother was a ruddy woman who looked much younger than her sixty years. She spoke of the local bears as if they were neighbors. She told me that a large male grizzly owned the mountain we were on. She said the female grizzly on her side of the lake had already arrived for the summer with her cubs and that she'd leave us alone. However, the male had a bad attitude toward guests.

I have only theories why the bear never came while the students were there; I was young and just starting to learn. When the season was over and the students had gone home, we began to break camp. Someone had to remain for the last weekend alone, while the others took one load to town. I stayed. The first morning, I walked out of camp toward some woods at base of the mountain. I was checking to be sure all the snares that we had set were taken down. I was drawn closer to the trees and soon saw fresh paw prints—prints so huge that I could have fit three of my large boots in the depression. I followed until they headed up the mountain.

The grandson stopped by later in the day and confirmed it was that big grizzly. The next day, I climbed the mountain to find the bear. When I got above the tree line, I just kept walking. I knew he was there. He ran from me; I found droppings that were still steaming.

That summer, I learned that I had power over the bear. We need not fear animals. We are here as shepherds over this creation. The reason some people are attacked is mainly fear-based. Fear can inspire you to set your energy field and stay strong in the face of an animal, but it can also create terror that will prevent you from keeping your energy egg energized. When an animal sees your energy field is in disarray, scattered, or unbalanced due to fear, it is confused and can become fearful. This can spark an attack. Nature strives for balance, and when a wild animal sees an oddity, such as a human with a strange energy field, it attacks, as it would any peculiar behavior. Or it attacks out of fear of this human that behaves impotently. Therefore, set your defense, and keep fear under control.

To protect yourself, avoidance is a perfect self-defense technique. Wolverines are perhaps the most vicious animals on the planet, and I survived an encounter with one while I was fast asleep (perhaps with the help of angels). Getting between a female bear and her cubs pushes the case for energy self-defense. You can avoid getting caught in these situations by using scanning and avoiding techniques.

The energy crystals are very exciting to utilize in the outdoors, and using the primary (or all three) is very in tune with nature. Be aware that wildlife may be drawn to your energy but will not harm you if they see you in such power. Even with just the primary crystal (which is a huge achievement), you will find it an enhancement over a healthy energy egg. The crystal will enhance your energy field and radiate Mother energy directly to your chakras, auras, mind, and body.

Animal energy is fascinating to experience:

As I was hiking along the Niagara Escarpment, I scanned for humans and then for a fox family that lived near a swamp. The male was usually prowling for food, while the female stayed with the cubs. I stood on the ridge at my favorite lookout, scanning the valley. I saw the families of foxes, humans, and squirrels. I couldn't find the male fox, so I scanned more intently. At that point, I could see all the life, from insects to birds. Where was the male fox? Was he hurt? I finally gave up. As I turned to leave, there he was, a few feet from me. He knew what I was doing. He stayed for a while and then trotted away down the path.

Hawk has come to me, as has eagle, dove, duck, and so many others. Different members of these families of birds have shown themselves to me, flying close or suddenly arriving in my view or startling me with a close encounter. When a type of bird comes into my sight or energy, I pay attention and decipher the meaning. What is Mother Earth telling me? Ted Andrews's book works well for me as a basis to find the obvious and, less so, messages. Mother Earth wants us to see, love, and feel all of creation. It's fun to place your hand on an animal's track and know what it was thinking, what it was doing, where it was going, how its health is, and so on. This is an enlightening and a powerful tool. It can be used to help heal a forest and align its energy, and it also helps you on your path.

Let the animals and birds teach you; they have so many lessons. You could build a home like a squirrel if you're caught in the woods in the winter. From the desert mouse, you can learn to drink the dew off rocks in the early morning. If you're in a survival situation, animals will come to you. When Natives need food, they ask for the deer, and in spirit the deer appears and gives itself.

ASTROLOGY

The universe is darkness and light. Our planet, the galaxy, and the universe are made up of dualities, light and dark being a fundamental duality. There is so much we can't see or fathom.

The Milky Way is a spiral of light and a spiral of darkness. In this spiral galaxy, energy fields tend to flow in spirals, like water down a drain. The energy entering and running down the cones at each chakra point does so in spirals. Proper flow of energy through our fields at rest can be seen as spirals. Using spiraling energy for releasing works well during healing.

Astrology shows us that the wisdom of the planets and cosmos affects us at the time of our incarnation into the physical world. A personal astrological study can reveal much about a person, and it's a worthwhile effort. However, I struggle with the infinite number of variables. For instance, Neptune has influence, but so do its moons. Where do we stop the analysis? I greatly identify with my sun and moon signs. I feel the effect of a Mercury retrograde and so on, but the level of complexity is more than my finite brain can process. My thoughts and observations are just a glimpse into the vast study of how the cosmos affects us.

If Mother Earth is our main life-giving energy source in the galaxy, then other planetary bodies also would affect us. Astrologers study that effect. The sun sign is the main astrological phenomenon usually cited. For instance, I'm a Scorpio with my moon in Cancer, and so on for all the planets out to Pluto (Scorpio being ruled by Mars and Pluto). There are many excellent astrologers available on the web: Marguerite Manning and Susan Miller are excellent sources.

We are complex beings. I believe I brought issues from past lives, so it's difficult for me to fathom all the reasons why I am who I am. I also believe that our planet and humans have become out of balance. I believe I'm here, with other light-beings, to bring balance and more light. Through remote viewing, I've discovered other planets with life. If you wish, you can see them too.

EXTRATERRESTRIAL LIFE

Remote viewing is essentially limitless. Many of my clients have had extraterrestrial experiences that impacted their energy eggs. I believe it's arrogant to assume that we're the only sentient beings in the entire universe.

The following was one occurrence:

A dear person came to me, concerned over the Zetas (an alien race that speaks through a woman in the United States). At the time, these aliens told the woman, telepathically, that a Planet X was going to fly near Earth. They gave exact dates and times. The aliens predicted areas of the earth that would be affected and recommended relocation instructions. The Zetas' earlier predictions regarding other events had all been correct, and purportedly the military around the world were taking it somewhat seriously. My friend was stressed about it, so I agreed to remote-view the Zetas.

I discovered that Zetas existed but were (fortunately for us) mistaken. Planet X existed, but the Zetas had miscalculated. Due to their incredibly high intellect, the Zetas' ego led them to overlook data. God (the One) was giving them a check to their ego. They failed to consider the impact that more than seven billion souls would have on the Planet X. The Zetas are mainly scientific and logical in their thinking processes, and they failed to see that the human collective conscious had an effect.

All this was done using remote viewing. Remote viewing is not limited to between Toledo, Ohio, and Prague, for instance.

Climate Change

At the time of this writing, climate change is an issue that deeply impacts us all. It seems to be a real phenomenon, given the droughts, floods, fires, freezing, and so on that follow no predicted weather patterns. However, our accumulation of weather data spans very few centuries.

I understand this cycle to be a manifestation due to a number of events. Overpopulation, overfarming, and overuse of the planet, in general, are important issues. Having the energy and force of over seven billion souls on a planet is another sizable issue. Outside forces and other effects (outside the parameters of this book) are part of the matter. We also have dark entities and humans who like to play on our fears. Humans with money and power have been playing God for centuries. Mother Earth is reacting to and acting on these and many other factors. (This would be best explained in a separate book on the topic I brushed on above regarding the Zetas; that other planets affect us.) I believe we can get through this time, but as a collective, we need to decide what our future will be. We are in control as stewards over this great land.

Let us act responsibly with our energy fields toward others, the planet, and the universe.

We must preserve our planet. This planet could be such a better place to live. We could solve overpopulation by dealing with our fears. Chemicals have made it possible for huge yields from the land so that we are no longer as in touch with the earth as we used to be and need to be. Genetic altering and abusing our scientific power has pushed us even further away.

We are a part of Earth, and Mother Earth gives us the power of life. We need to get back to the source of heaven and earth energy. I've had the privilege of working all across Canada, in the United States, Europe, and the Middle East. Our world is vast and the variety of life astounding. We humans must find gentle peace with ourselves and our great Mother Earth to discover hope for a bright future. It's out there for us.

CHAPTER 9

PRACTICE MAKES PERFECT

We can all perform the skills I've described in this book. As children, we read energy fields and auras, telepathically communicated, and saw and spoke with angels.

We're all born with a high level of emotional intelligence, but I believe we're also born with an even higher level of spiritual intelligence. This makes meeting strangers much easier, since we can tell if they are light-workers or not. Children are clear readers. If my energy is up, a child will smile; if I turn negative, the child will frown because the light is gone. I once stood near an infant in his mother's arms, and the child smiled. Then, someone very negative for me entered the room, and my energy shut off. The baby was confused. The look on his face said, "Where did you go?"

You may be familiar with the innate skills that all children have, including my own:

My three preschool children were watching TV while I sat behind them, meditating. My daughter felt something, and she turned and said, "Dad, what are you doing?" I opened my eyes and said, "Why? What do you see?" She said, "You're all blue!" I told her to watch and wait, and I intensified the energy. Then she said, "Now you're white ... now blue! Why are you fooling around?"

When my children were small, we'd walk in the woods together. My daughter would spot animals that were invisible to me. When I asked where they were and what she saw, she'd point at the thick brush and say, "In there, Dad. A squirrel, and it's all blue." Sure enough, a squirrel popped out. She could see the creature's energy field through the foliage. If she examined a feather, she'd see a faint glow that would fade with time. The color varied with the mood of the person or animal. Intense action brought on a brighter color and was associated with the main chakra that was activated. I personally give off a yellow glow most often (associated with perceiving the outside world and my past trauma, all solar plexus) and blue when I am talking to angels and so on.

My boys, identical twins, had a special bond and would always know where the other was, even if something separated them. I'd ask one where the other was and, even if he was focused on something else, he'd point directly at the invisible brother, directly through whatever separated them.

At my first parent-teacher interview when my daughter was in junior kindergarten, the teacher showed us her workbooks. At first, my daughter had drawn herself silly, with purple hair. The teacher had corrected her, and now she was drawing herself properly, with blonde hair and clothes. I was furious, though I said nothing—and I was happy at the same time! In the first drawing, my daughter had drawn her body with all seven chakras colored correctly. Even the indigo and violet were correct. How amazing! But the school had taught her that her sight was a lie. They denied her vision and forced her to shut it down.

When my daughter drew that picture, did I try to change the system? Did I take her out of the school and place her somewhere more conducive to promoting her incredible gift? No. I fell into society's mold. We're born with the ability to see auras, angels, chakras, and much more. But this is taught out of us. We're ridiculed and told we're wrong until we believe the lie. Don't do this. Embrace what you really are. Embrace your true nature.

Other cultures acknowledge the mystic realm. You will find the Orthodox Church embraces mysticism more readily than Western Catholicism. Hindi embrace energy and nature; Buddhism is extremely connected—the list goes on. It is interesting that Western culture has generally less mysticism, yet there seems to be a healthy shift of late. It is not uncommon in North America to say the energy seems off when referring to a place or person. Many cultures acknowledge that seeing in the angelic realm is natural, healthy, and our gift. I hope, as humans, we can get back to what we were as children.

In my workshops, I try to show people how simple energy work really is. As adults, we can reverse and relearn what was lost. We can develop incredible skills in the area of energy and mystical awareness. If all of us, including world leaders, could learn again how to see in this realm, the world would be a better place to live.

One of the greatest hurdles to developing your intuition is fear. As Franklin D. Roosevelt said, "Let me assert my firm belief that the only thing we have to fear is fear itself; nameless, unreasoning, unjustified terror which paralyzes needed efforts to convert retreat into advance."[4]

Many of my clients claim to have had amazing psychic experiences as children but were unable to recapture the skill as adults. Part of the reason for this lack is conditioning from themselves and society, but mostly it's because something terrified them as children, causing them to stop playing with the ability. If no adult trained or guided them, they were unable to try again or progress.

I give my workshop students two pieces of advice regarding lost abilities:

1. They must honor their instinct to stop this kind of activity. They were freaked out and they stopped. With training, they must realize they're safe and can function in the spirit realm with protection, both from their own angels and the High Lord.
2. They must realize that they have an on/off switch that will aid them and keep them healthy. We can't be in the spirit realm permanently, for we've decided to be in our physical bodies, the here and now. Realize that any time you wish to stop, you can turn the ability off, just as you did as a child.

As children, we were born with a strong sense of integrity. We should cherish and protect the purity of sight and mind that children have. Children can readily see energy, angels, and so much in the realm that most adults ignore. It's difficult for our planet to progress and survive when we (and our leaders) aren't regularly communicating with angels and higher beings. Have the courage to stay in your integrity. Find that purity you had as a child. Become innocent once more.

In this book, I've tried to explain how to perform a number of skills. The best way to progress is to relax, take a deep breath, and just let it

---

[4] Franklin D. Roosevelt, Inaugural Address, March 4, 1933.

happen. It will come to you. As I said, you could do these things—and more—as a child.

In some areas (maybe all), you will exceed me. But don't judge or criticize yourself if there is a lack of progress. Being stuck is just part of the process. The more you work with energy, the more these elements will become second nature and instinctive. Learn to trust your feelings and intuition. Let them guide you. I believe we all have a path and free will to choose, but the High Lord has a plan for our lives. I pray I can live with awareness, the grace of the High Lord, and Mother Earth, so I can follow my path.

I encourage you to stay in the light and practice holy works. It will make the path easier. Avoid shortcuts, but realize the duality that it takes discipline, effort, and time, but you can acquire knowledge in an instant!

Relax, and remember that you already have the skills; you just need to remember them. Have fun! If you think you've done something dangerous, come back to you, be present, set your fields, call angels, and pray. You'll be fine.

Bless you.

APPENDIX

EXERCISES

The exercises have been kept generally in the same order in which they appear in the book, with editing and more detail. The first four exercises read at first as the main text but have additional information at the end of each; these are the lessons to master foremost. This appendix is meant as a reference; including the entire exercise will prevent the need to flip back and forth to the main text. The exercises build on each other for the most part and consequently are not in alphabetical order. It would be imprudent, for instance, to have angel channeling at the top when it is one of the most advanced skills, requiring mastery of energy self defense. To ease the task of searching, here is the sequence: Feel the Energy; Scan Chakras; Sense the Energy Egg; Change Your Energy Egg; Create Space; Power (Energy) Crystals; Energy Field around a Campsite; Energy Field around Your Children; Meditation; The Healing Session; Create an Energy Self-Defense Shield; Crystal Defense; Remote Viewing and Angel Channeling.

FEEL THE ENERGY

This exercise is to activate your hands for energy flow. The centre of your palms is the main areas for the flow and perception of energy. By holding the palms facing each other, one foot apart, you should feel energy pulsing in both hands. This is an energy ball. As you move your palms closer, the feeling should intensify and decrease when moved apart.

If you are just beginning and have trouble feeling energy with your hands, spread your arms out wide, and then slowly bring your arms closer together in front of your body. At a few feet apart you will feel a tingle in your palms. If not, then focus on the earth energy flowing up your feet and the sky energy flowing through your head, and try again moving your arms together in front of your chest.

You will begin to feel a pulse of energy. Pay attention as it grows in intensity until you have an energy ball between your hands. This is a bundle of energy that you will feel in the palms of your hands. It should feel more intense the closer your hands get to each other.

If one person can do this and another cannot, then the first person should hold her hands close to the other person. The person aiding the other should hold her hands outside her partner's hands, adding energy. Keep sending energy to the other person until she begins to feel the pulse.

If you are on your own, use the crystal between your hands to feel the energy. Move your hands farther and farther away, then closer, and then away from the crystal, and repeat until you feel the energy between your palms without the crystal. The crystal is energizing your hands.

If you are missing an arm (amputee), then use the crystal to form a ball between your hand and the crystal. The exercises below can be done with one hand, imagination, and patience.

Play with the ball by expanding and contracting it with hand movements. Run it up and over your body or over your partner's body. Use your imagination; the purpose is to allow and ignite the energy flowing in and out of your palms. Once you have played for a while, take a break and come back to ensure you can reactivate it. Play some more. Then you are ready to move to the next exercise below.

(If you're working with energy crystals, use the primary crystal around your body and set a small one in each of your hands. This will activate this functionality.)

SCAN CHAKRAS

Stand at the side of your partner with the front of your body facing her side and stretch your arms out, one behind her body and one in front. Hold your hands about six inches away from her body along a vertical center line. Move your hands up and down the center line, six inches from her body, following the line connecting the chakras.

The goal is to pick up or feel where the chakras are by sensing the energy pulse in the palms of your hands. Stop at each chakra to feel the energy, and you can move around the chakra to feel the difference. Be aware you may feel pulsing in other areas due to issue, injury, or healthy vibrant tissue, but the chakras should be identifiable and strong.

Then, let your partner do the same for you. If the Feel the Energy exercise worked, this part should be easy. If it is not, go back to the Feel the Energy exercise to really ensure you feel it. Then try this one again. Go back and forth until you have it and before moving on to the next lesson.

If you are on your own, use alternate hands to scan the front of your body, six inches away, up and down your vertical center line that connects all the chakras.

SENSE THE ENERGY EGG

Stand fifteen to twenty feet away from your partner. Point your hands at the other person and slowly move closer toward her until you feel a shift of energy in your hands or your energy field, and then stop. This is the meeting point of the outer edge of your energy egg and your partner's energy egg—your seventh auras. This is where your energy eggs touch.

Now return to your original places and have the other person repeat the above, slowly walking toward her. Then discuss what you felt and experienced. Now repeat with the first person but when your energy eggs meet, stop, observe your feelings, and then continue to move toward your partner. Stop when you feel an additional pop or increase in energy. This should be where your energy egg meets her physical body, or her energy egg hits your body (depending on which one is held further out). Now continue to move closer until your energy egg encompasses her physical body; note the difference. Return to your place and let your partner practice moving in.

Relax, breathe, and try it again to see if you can change the size of your egg.

If working alone, hold your hands toward your crystal and walk toward it. Stop when you feel a shift (at between three and thirty feet). This is the outer edge of your energy egg meeting the crystal.

Additionally, if you can see energy, try perceiving the energy egg, energy core, and all the auras. See the main energy beam from sky and earth and also the two beams interwoven, one up the right leg the other down, crossing at the thymus, as described in chapter 1. (You can also feel for these two energy beams.)

CHANGE YOUR ENERGY EGG

Practice pulling in and moving out your seventh aura, the edge of your energy egg. Stand fifteen feet away from your partner (or crystal, if alone). Bring in and push out energy inside your egg. This is best accomplished with breath. Inhale and exhale three times slowly. Now imagine your egg pulling in (or pushing out), and breathe in and out, letting go of the desire to push out while still imagining it going out. Your partner may feel the difference immediately, but have her walk toward you, and see if your egg did draw in (or out).

Use breath, and let go of forcing the egg, just allow it to move in and out.

Practice bringing it in as tightly as possible and pushing out as far as you like. Realize this is tiring work, and even the smallest movement on your first day of attempting this is a huge accomplishment. It will take practice for you to make major shifts. Go easy.

And alone you can use the crystal by pulling in and moving toward it to feel if it shifted.

Work with your loved ones and see how you can change the way you hold your energy field.

CREATE SPACE

To create space around a healing room, begin by standing in the center of the room. Energize your egg and outer aura by bringing earth energy up and sky energy down. Focus on this beam and, if you can, the other two interwoven beams (one up the right leg crossing at the thymus and out the left side of your head, and the other down and opposite). These two opposing yet balanced beams aid in your intuition and perception.

Push out your outer aura as in the exercise above (Change Your Energy Egg) until it has the shape of your room. It can take on a cube-type shape. Now say in your mind or out loud, "Stay around my room." Pull back in your egg, and try to sense if the shell remains around your room. Leave the room, and walk away; then approach it once you are thirty feet (or so) away. Your egg should contact the shell around your room. It should feel like when you worked with a person or the crystal.

Leave the space and remain away for a few hours. Return, sensing for the shell again. If it is not there, repeat the exercise, this time sensing if there are surrounding negative energies that would have hampered you. If so, you will require a defensive shield of mirrors or another type. (Refer to Create an Energy Self-Defense Shield or Crystal Shield, below.) It may be that you have to practice more on a smaller room or just try again. Work more with energizing of your energy field before a third attempt. It will come to you with practice.

(If working with the three energy crystals, the second crystal can be set around any space on ground level. The third can be expanded easily and left in place as the most effective shield. See Crystal Defense.)

POWER (ENERGY) CRYSTALS

How do you obtain them? I was given the first crystal in May 2008. Then, when I had learned much (though a fraction of the total), I was given the second. Months passed before I obtained the third. My intentions had to be pure and integrity sure. Through mediation, allowing, self-healing, and patience, Mother gave them to me. As you work more with energy, your field, and your intention, they will come to you.

Be mindful that this is an extremely advanced skill and receiving the crystals may take years of practicing with your energy field and improving intuition. That said, some may acquire them sooner. I have shown them to clients and fellow energy practitioners who were able to receive the primary immediately, but please do not judge yourself if the timing for you is years away.

Sit alone in a quiet room. You can add candles and incense and surround yourself with crystals, as you wish. Create space, and then focus on each chakra and then each aura, one at a time. Be with each until it feels whole and in balance. Connect with Mother and Father, and see all three beams of energy at your core. Dip into those streams.

Then say out loud, "Great Mother, please send me the primary crystal for your highest intent. I ask with all purity, courage, and integrity." Relax, and wait to receive.

When all three are received (which may take years), remember that the primary naturally extends vertically, with the top at your egg above the crown and at the egg below your feet, while the egg is at its natural, relaxed state. The main primary crystal is elongated along the vertical axis. The second is a cylinder, and the main primary touches the inside of the secondary cylinder, digging in a bit. If you have primary crystals at all your chakras, they attach naturally to the main primary crystal. The third or tertiary crystal will come up from earth and then follow the cylinder of the secondary and can glide up and down, sending power to all your centers, but will rest at the heart, or sacral chakra, as you wish or need.

As a side note, if you are a crystalline conscience technique (CCT) practitioner, you will find your experience enhanced by these crystals, based on my experience at a CCT Level 1.

ENERGY FIELD AROUND A CAMPSITE

Protection while wilderness camping is similar to the Create Space exercise. Sit in your tent or stand at the center of the campsite, and create space around the tent or group of tents. Walk outside the shell and test it by walking toward the shell and feeling it strike your egg. (If you see energy, look for earth and sky energy as a beam. The interwoven beams may not be present, and that is because they are part of a creature, not a space. If you do allow them in your created space, be aware you have left more of your limitless essence at that space, thus increasing its effectiveness.)

Return to the center of the shell. This next shell can be created in the same way or you can try something more advanced. Imagine the space surrounding your campsite out to one mile away. (If you can remote view, then view this area.) Now, all at the same time, call in sky energy and earth energy, and breathe in and then out as you energize your egg and pop a shield into place, a mile out from your site. This is similar to everything you've learned—an allowing, imagining, and yet intending action. If the pop does not work, create the one-mile shell using Create Space.

It is best not to make the one-mile shell a full defensive space since it will disrupt energy and life in such a wide area. With intent, scan this shell and feel it. Say out loud, "This is not intended to block but to alert me." Set the intention to have it alert you, even when asleep, if something threatening passes through. This will challenge your intuitive abilities. If this does not seem to work, then just set it at a weaker energy level, and it will work in a similar fashion (it will normally be weaker due to its size, so you may be able to leave it as first created).

If you want to test this shell, then walk out the mile. The advantage to having others with you is they can stand outside the first shell you made and test it, and they also can scan and sense for the shield a mile out. If one of them has remote viewing capability, that person can test your shells.

ENERGY FIELD AROUND YOUR CHILDREN

This exercise assumes the child is your own or one that you have guardianship over. There would be moral and integrity issues if you did this for someone's children without permission.

This differs from other forms of defense, as the others described are self-defense. You can protect anyone inside your Create Space, Energy or Crystal Self-Defense Shield. An energy field around a child is without you. Unlike putting a space around your car or healing room, this is a living human. The work is intimate.

There are two methods. The first involves doing a Create Space around the child while you are next to him or her and asking the shell to follow the child and stay. It will stay if you have the child's permission.

Alternately, you can hold the child on your lap or sit beside her or him on the floor. Energize your energy egg, and connect clearly with divine (Father Sky and Mother Earth energies and the energy core stream that flows root to crown, crown to root). Feel your egg around the child, and feel the child's energy egg. In your mind, say, *Please allow me to shield and protect you*. Purposely add your energy core stream to the child's, and energize her or his energy egg using your energy. Let your energy flow to the outer aura of the girl or boy. Set an energy defense outside the child's egg, and slowly break the energy contact, intending all your energy to leave the little one's energy core stream and empower the protective shield.

MEDITATION

I will describe two types of meditation.

Sit in a quiet room at a quiet time. Do it in silence first and then later with music. Close your eyes, and focus on an imaginary ball of light at your heart or third-eye chakra. You could focus on the sky or earth energy that enters your energy egg or the two interwoven shafts at your energy core. Calm your breathing, and go into the light. Try to fill your mind with just that light. Concentrate on nothing but the light. Once your mind is filled with light, imagine unconditional love. What would it be like? Would it look like the light? Imagine the light is that love. Go into the light and imagine what unconditional love feels like. Focus on the light and the love.

Once the above is mastered for even just a few moments, you can take the ball of light and imagine it moving all around your body. Place it where there is discomfort and where there is not. Move it to all your chakras or wherever, but when you are near the end of the meditation, move it back to where it began, at the heart or third eye (or wherever), and slowly come out of the light.

The oak leaf was a focus of mine. The purpose of meditation is to focus and arrive at a state of no mind. By sitting quietly, focusing on just the leaf, I slowly reached a point—after repeated attempts—of filling all my thought and mind on this wondrous specimen of divine perfection. Then, as my mind only had one thing, one thought, it was easy to transform to no thought.

Sitting with the leaf, I studied it and memorized its shape and then all the veins and lines. I focused on the irregularities and imperfections. After three sessions it was memorized, yet more aspects became clear until I could see each subtle detail, and then I began to perceive its infinite and divine perfection. By the tenth session, focusing on just the leaf, I could begin to dip into the void of no mind. No leaf, no one, and no thought. And the trance would deeply soothe and heal me.

As you start, it will be difficult to concentrate. If you lose concentration do not worry or judge; just come back to the leaf. Then, slowly it will get easier, and the length of your meditations will seem shorter, though they grow. Be very patient and kind as you learn because many personal issues will surface as you gain focus. I am a student of mediation, and it is a life study for many, so even if you achieve a millisecond of *no mind*, you will have succeeded, and the reward for you and your energy field will be magnificent. The reward is very individual, but peace, love, and forgiveness lie out there to be found.

The Healing Session (General Treatment)

This is for a healing treatment for general relaxation and alignment, where specific injured areas are not targeted. This can be done exclusively or after particular injured areas were worked on, as described in chapter 3.

Be aware of the client's comfort level and query the client as you proceed. It is easiest to work on someone while lying clothed on a portable massage table, but they can sit in a comfortable chair. You will need a stool. Ensure you are both comfortable.

Begin by placing your hands on her head (this can be over both ears or forehead and back of head). Leave them on the head for a few minutes (longer if there are issues here), and then move to the feet. Place one hand on the top and the other on the bottom, back, or the ankle (your choice) of each foot. Hold this for a few minutes. Then hold both feet, one in each hand, for five minutes. (Given that two interwoven beams reside inside the main energy beam, you may feel energy going more downward in the left foot and upward for the right.)

Now return to her head and place the hands on the forehead and back of head. After a few minutes, move the hand at the back to back of the neck. After a few minutes, put both hands on the tops of the shoulders. Then move to one side, and place one hand on the front and back of the shoulder, then the elbow, then hand, and repeat on the opposite shoulder, holding for a few minutes at each spot.

Place one hand on the center line of the chest but high up. If possible, place the other on the back, directly behind the first. Hold for a few minutes. (This should be the thymus, and if you see energy, ensure the two interwoven beams cross here. If not, allow them; place energy into aligning them.) Then move to the center of the chest, then the diaphragm area, and then stomach. Finally, move to the middle of the abdomen, just above the navel.

Now hold both hands four inches above the pelvis and then move to the groin. Then place both hands around the middle of one thigh and then the knee, shin, and last, the foot. Repeat on the other side. Hold one foot in one hand and the other with another. You may perceive the two superimposed beams, one flowing up the right leg and the other down the left. Hold this for five minutes. While at one side standing midway, wave your hands above the person in a flowing pattern and make pushing motions toward the feet, as if you were forcing the air down. This cleanses the auras.

The person will feel relaxed and may need to lie or sit still for a while before getting up.

CREATE AN ENERGY SELF-DEFENSE SHIELD

Two types of shield will be described. The first is a shield surrounding you at a distance beyond your energy egg, miles or feet away. The second is defending your energy egg, Be aware Create Space will block almost all attacks directed at your space, especially if you are inside the space. It is best to be aware of your energy core, including the main shaft and the two interwoven beams.

For the first type of defense, you create space as above (in Create Space) or as you have done in Energy Field around a Campsite. When an attack comes toward the shield (if your intuition tells you it is coming or you see via remote viewing), cover the outside of the sphere with mirrors pointing outward. If you expect the attack to come or you wish to rest, then place the mirrors and leave them. Mirrors will block 90 percent of attacks that your normal Create Space would not block, which means 99 percent of all attacks normally encountered. All of the possible coverings described in the defense of your energy egg, below, can be applied to this defensive shell. First, strengthen your outer aura with light. If battling with the occult, demons, or corporate nonlight collectives, the attacks can be more than just pure energy and can take on creative forms.

Overcoming most of these attacks still involves the outer aura/ seventh chakra. For hooks, lining the outside of the egg with steel prevents their digging in. As said before, if it's dark jelly, make your outer shell like Teflon so it slides off. If it's sludge, bring up earth energy fire to burn it. If an energy dragon is used, ask Mother Earth to send a dragon. A diamond outer shield, however, would work. For persistent attacks, you should push back, out past your egg. Someone who is relentless to disturb you may require an energy push to stop him, but most people will stop soon, based on a solid defense. Your imagination is the best defense in these rare occasions.

The auras are all vital to energy self-defense. The main focus is the outer aura to stop attacks from penetrating and entering the egg. The sixth and second auras are linked to the sacral and third eye, gaining power directly from the power chakra and the mind. The sixth directly supports the seventh. The second aura surrounds the physical body with support from the same chakras as the sixth and can stiffen to protect the body.

As said before, the fourth aura is most affiliated with the heart chakra and unconditional love. Love is the primary defense, and the heart and fourth chakra support all as a bulwark to attack. Enhancing your energy field further is the first aura, protecting the vital organs and epicenters of the chakras. Gaining power directly from the energy core, this is a tough barrier for an energy attack. The third and fifth auras perceive and decipher the attack and create elasticity to the overall defense. These two bend inward and flex as required, adding a different type of strength, much as steel can flex. Energizing these and all the auras is required for complete defense, and with these two chakras energized, facing fear (solar plexus chakra) and guarding your expression (throat chakra) is the path to peace and harmony required for that perfect self-defense shield. Being relaxed in a self-defense situation is important and can be achieved with practice.

You can attract antilight workers while remote viewing. They may follow you or attack you on the view or projection. The best defense is to end the view or projection and come back to your protective shell (you always set this up prior to viewing or projecting). Once back, follow the techniques above in the Create Space exercise. If you are grabbed or prevented from returning in some way (extremely rare event), give up, release the need to return, and let go as you did when manipulating your energy egg at the very first exercises. This will release you from them. Then run in a random course back to your energy defense.

CRYSTAL DEFENSE (OR THE ULTIMATE SELF-DEFENSE)

The following assumes you can utilize the crystals as in Power Crystal and have remote viewing abilities (or a strong imagination). Be aware that the crystals will come one at a time in the described order. Always place the primary before calling the secondary, and only call the third when the two are in place. You need not worry since a crystal will not come if the prerequisite is not in place. As you work more with them, they will naturally be in place in your energy field at all times and will be there when required or requested.

Create space around you, and add the primary crystal (large and extending from top to bottom of your egg, engulfing your energy core and most of your physical body). Your outer aura will be charged. Now remote-view or project inside the crystal. Immediately, your mind, body, and egg will be supercharged. The crystal will seem to bulge. This first stage will already place you in a better defense mode than the Self Defense Shield, above.

If you have the secondary crystal, pull it up from earth while you are viewing inside the first crystal. You will now have the two locked together. This will increase your defense to a new height that is virtually impregnable. You can come out of the primary when you want and go back in as you like. The secondary crystal should have your egg inside, and your outer aura will not be touched by negative energies.

The crystals automatically become impermeable to energy flow when that flow is unhealthy and negative for you. All you need to do is ask for them and receive, and they will function for defense. Remote viewing inside the primary just enhances their ability, which will work if you cannot or choose not to. Realize that the crystal's natural state is not impregnability but as a filter, conveyor, and catalyst of energy.

The third crystal is a many-sided sphere that, when relaxed, sits at the sacral, cradled by the primary crystal. The crystal will swell if the outer aura or secondary crystal contacts negative energy. (The secondary crystal often pulls in toward the energy core to energize it.) For defense, and if the two lower crystals are activated to defend, the third crystal will swell out beyond the second. Remote view or astral project into the third power crystal (or imagine doing so), and it will push out against the negative energies, beating them back easily. The sphere can then be left enclosing the entire energy egg until the attack is abated. You can move in and out with the first and third as you wish, if the attack persists.

I have found using these crystals for defense is far superior to pure energy defense but energy defense is highly effective on its own. The more you work with energy and purity, the more you will be open to receive the crystals. Once you have them, they never leave. They always will be in your quiver as tools for all you do.

The third crystal can be expanded to fill your space, as you did with your outer aura in Create Space. A crystal can be left here for a far more effective protective shell. When you leave, Mother will give you another tertiary crystal. If at ground level, leave a secondary crystal for a very solid protective shell. This second crystal is as effective for defense and is not as easily seen by remote viewers.

Please note: Defense is only one attribute of the crystals. These have so many uses as to be limitless. Healing, artistry, intuition, music, sexuality, all senses, clarity, math, science, and virtually every aspect of life is enhanced by and with them.

REMOTE VIEWING (THIS HAS BEEN TAKEN FROM THE MAIN TEXT FOR REFERENCE PURPOSES.)

Before conducting a remote view and certainly before astral projecting, you must have mastered the skill of Create Space and Create an Energy Self-Defense Shield or Crystal Shield. Create space and ensure that the energy around your place is solid and strong. Spend time concentrating on that shield and your strong outer aura. If you don't believe you're in a place of strength, wait for another time to begin. Call in angels as added protection, and use energy crystals. Clear your energy fields as much as possible.

Once your safe space is created, relax and imagine a bird—any kind of bird—sitting on your shoulder. This imagined bird will be the vehicle for your viewing, the focus of your energy and mind. Focus on this bird, and imagine it as real. Relax, breathe, and look through the eyes of the bird. Once you can see through its eyes, allow the bird to fly around the room and perch wherever you wish. Do this a few times until you feel in control of the bird. This energy bird is a part of you in bird-energy form. Now, let the bird fly out of your space. Fly out over the area around the building you are in and view the landscape. You also can scan the area for energies, to see the different energy fields created by people and nature. Open your mind to all possibilities.

Bring the bird back close to your space, and ask if it was followed. If the answer is yes, ask your angels to chase away the energy. If it is human energy, you may need to push it back to where it came from and then return to your safe space. As you do this, watch for undesirable humans who may track your movements. If your space is secure, you need not fear. As a light-worker, you will be safe. When your bird is safely back, relax, breathe, and end the session. A clap of your hands will do nicely.

You can then physically walk or drive around your area to discover if what you saw in your remote view was accurate. Did you see a community event at a park in your viewing, and is it actually there? You could set up with a friend to be outside doing an action unknown to you, remote view it, and then call and describe what she was doing. When I was first learning, I'd find an event or out-of-the-ordinary sight and later walk or drive there to verify the accuracy. This helps build confidence.

After about five scans of the area around your space, venture further afield. Start moving the bird faster, and you will begin to view without the bird, but if you ever struggle to view, come back to using the energy bird. It works every time.

To make it easier, another person can work with you. Be sure you're both protected. The protective shield can be with both of your energy fields. You can verify what you see when you leave your space with your partner. In that way, you qualify your experience (but it's not necessary). With another person, you'll be able to tell the difference between imagining and actual viewing. The best way to discern and learn is to experiment.

It is easiest to remote view on a person you know. The connection you have with that person is real and will aid you in seeing. Set up a session with a person you trust who is miles away, and ask that person to wear a shirt or clothes he or she normally would not wear, or have the person do something different, such as dance. Now try to see the person, and contact him or her later. Be aware that if you are communicating with the person electronically while remote-viewing, it will probably interfere with the connection. I suggest viewing the person and then waiting to confirm the accuracy, as remote viewing does not follow time perfectly—what you see may be moments in the near future.

ANGEL CHANNELING

Caution: Do not attempt the following exercise unless Create an Energy Self-Defense or Crystal Defense and remote viewing have been accomplished. You must be able to clearly see and communicate with angels.

Complete a Create Space and then an Energy or Crystal Self-Defense on the room you occupy. If other humans are in your space, their physical and energy fields must be outside your energy egg, and they must ensure that the eggs never touch during the channeling. The space must have a minimum of seven angels outside and seven inside, in addition to the one to be channeled; the angel you are to channel will guarantee that enough angels are present. Only the angel to be channeled will be in your egg. Your outer-aura protection must be at its maximum light-energy level and at its natural distance from your physical body. (The energy crystals can be engaged for your egg as well as the space.)

To channel an angel, follow these steps. You must have the purest intent and highest purpose, with consummate approval. Read over the instructions a number of times until they are memorized before proceeding with the channeling.

- Center your awareness clearly on your energy field and the flow of energy from root and crown.
- Align your chakras by focusing on each, one at a time, and ensure the light is solid without any blockages.
- Focus specifically on the area inside your first aura (all three beams of energy).
- Ask the angel to be channeled to hover behind your head.
- Ask the angel for his or her name. If you do not clearly receive the name, do not continue.
- You will be required, in *a moment*, to open the back of your energy egg from the throat chakra (at the soft, lower back of your head) through the thymus to your heart chakra. This is done in a similar way to shifting your egg in and out from your body, a combination of intent and allowing. Imagine seeing the egg open at the back of your head and neck. This imagery will help you when it is time to open.
- Focus on your heart chakra and the fields up and back, from the heart center to the back of the head (the back of the throat chakra).
- The angel must hover behind your head.
- Say aloud, "I open my auras for our highest good, and I ask [*name of the angel*] to enter."
- Very quickly, open your egg (from the heart to throat chakra as described) and close it quickly!
- You should now have a beautiful, light-giving being of joy, love, and holiness inside your core.
- When the experience is over, or if at any time you are overwhelmed, say, "Go!" and the angel will depart. You won't need to purposely open your egg.

- Your egg will automatically close, and the flow of energy will be restored.
- When you're finished, double-check that no negative or other energies entered you. Then clear your energy field, and spend the next thirty minutes calming yourself from the experience.

Instructions for a second support person in the space while the channeling occurs:

- Center your awareness clearly on your energy field, the flow of energy from root and crown.
- Align your chakras by focusing on each, one at a time, and ensure the light is solid without any blockages.
- If you can create space, add your protection to the space. Use the crystals, if you can.
- If you can see and communicate with angels, bring more in the guard outside and inside the space but not inside the egg of the person channeling.
- You can send love and energy to the other person, but do not let your egg touch the other.

Channeling should be done only on rare occasions. This is ensured somewhat, since angels will refuse if you're not ready for the session. I like to combine channeling with a dietary detox so my body and fields are more prepared, and I have a clearer experience.

Much of the above energy-related exercises are sourced from Chinese (Tai Chi, Qigong), Tibetan, Shamanic, and other cultures.

GLOSSARY

angels: Ethereal beings of light, messengers of God. Refer to chapter 7 for more information.

astral projection: When a part of your essence leaves your energy field and is present in a remote location.

aura: Layers of energy inside and making up the energy egg. Refer to chapter 1 for a full description.

chakra: Energy center of a creature. Refer to chapter 1 for a full description.

channeling: Allowing an ethereal creature to enter your energy field. (Angel channeling revealed to me in November 1999.)

demons: Ethereal beings of light; followers of Lucifer and other fallen archangels.

distant healing: Healing someone who is outside your vision and surroundings (sending healing energy).

feel the energy: An acute tingling felling, sensation of heat, or flow of energy.

earth energy fire: Energy from Mother Earth that comes in form of fire to consume negative energy.

energy awareness: The ability to feel energy related to a person and his or her energy field.

energy ball: A perceived ball of energy that develops between the palms of two hands.

energy beams: Two beams of energy inside a person that are superimposed on and interwoven into the main energy core beam. One flows up and the other down. Refer to chapter 1 and the third diagram (revealed to me from the divine, April 2005).

energy bird: An ethereal object used for remote viewing.

energy blockages or blocks: Places where the natural flow of energy is interrupted.

energy core stream: The shaft of energy running vertically in the center of all living things that is made up of energy from the earth through the root chakra and energy from the universe through the crown chakra. (See Mother Earth and sky energy, below.) This shaft has two streams superimposed and interwoven. Refer to chapter 1.

energy crystals: The three power crystals revealed to me, beginning on May 17, 2008. These three crystals have multiple applications in healing, awareness, intuition, communing with angels, and energy defense, to name a few.

energy field or energy egg: The layers of auras around a being in egg shape that make up a defined area of energy.

energy flow: The flow of invisible energy that makes up the energy realm.

energy gate: A chakra that mainly receives energy from the outside world.

energy healing: Using energy transfer to remove energy blockages.

energy mirror: Ethereal mirror like energy structures that reflects energy in the energy realm.

energy pole: See energy core stream, above.

energy port: A chakra that mainly gives off energy to the outside world.

energy pulse: When feeling the energy is magnified and pulsated. Usually experienced while scanning or when energy is transferred.

energy realm: The dimension where invisible energy exists. All beings, substances, and planets give off and receive energy.

energy self-defense or energy defense: Blocking or defending against energies in the energy realm that are not visible to the normal human vision. The act of using your energy field (auras, chakras, and divine energy) to defend yourself from energy attacks. By energizing your energy field, you can be impervious to energy attacks, remote viewing, and astral projection.

energy sparring: For the purpose of learning, the act of sending energy at another person in the energy realm.

energy structure: A form in the energy realm that has substance in that realm.

energy transfer: Putting energy from one being into another or into a space.

energy-type attacks: Sending or receiving energy from another source that is unhealthy for the receiver.

exorcisms: The act of removing a demon from inside a person's energy field.

mind awareness: Being aware of what the mind is thinking, feeling, and how its energy is flowing.

Mother Earth: The conscious life force deep inside the earth and throughout the world that gives life to all living things and energy to all substances on the planet, gravity being one perception of that energy.

mystic realm: The dimension where angels, demons, and other corporeal and ethereal beings reside and interact with each other, the energy realm and the physical realm.

occult/cult: The practice of nonlight, antilight, or dark arts. Using human and other energies for negative purposes. Groups that practice these arts.

past-life regression: Seeing in your mind a life in the past, before this life, where your soul inhabited a different body.

power crystal: See energy crystal.

reading energy: Seeing in the energy realm.

Reiki: The Usui System of Natural Healing, as passed down from Mikao Usui to Phyllis Furumoto.

releasing: Allowing blockages in the energy field to leave.

remote viewing: When your mind's eye (the images you see inside your brain) leaps out from you so you can see distant places.

scan: The act of using your palms to pass over an area to feel the energy, or the act of remote viewing to look at the energy realm in the surrounding area.

see the energy: The ability to perceive energy in the energy realm.

sky energy (Father Sky): Energy that comes from Father into the crown chakra. Father is known as God, the One, High Lord, and many other names.

BIBLIOGRAPHY

Bowman, Carol. *Children's Past Lives: How Past Life Memories Affect Your Child*. New York: Bantam Books, 1997.

Frankl, Viktor E. *Man's Search for Meaning*. Boston: Beacon Press, 2006.

Rosenman, Samuel, ed. *The Public Papers of Franklin D. Roosevelt, Volume Two: The Year of Crisis, 1933*. New York: Random House, 1938.

Wiseman, Richard. *The Luck Factor*. London: Random House, 2003.

FURTHER READING

Morehouse, David. Psychic Warrior: The True Story of America's Foremost Psychic Spy and the Cover-Up of the CIA's Top-Secret Stargate Program. New York: St. Martin's Press, 1998.

—Excellent for understanding the body, digestion, and detoxification: Matsen, Jonn, Jeanne Marie Martin, and Nelson Dewey. *Eating Alive: Prevention Thru Good Digestion*. North Vancouver, B.C.: Crompton Books, 1988.

—The best book for understanding the spirits of animals, birds, and more:

Andrews, Ted. *Animal Speak: The Spiritual & Magical Powers of Creatures Great & Small*. St. Paul, Minn.: Llewellyn Publications, 1993.

—For tarot cards, I recommend the Connolly deck by Eileen Connolly and the following two books:

Connolly, Eileen. *Tarot A New Handbook for the Apprentice, Volume I of the Connolly Tarot*. North Hollywood, CA: New Castle Printing, 1990.

Connolly, Eileen. *Tarot A New Handbook for the Journeyman, Volume II of the Connolly Tarot*. North Hollywood, CA: New Castle Printing, 1987.

—A great set of books on the outdoors begins with:

Brown, Tom. *Tom Brown's Field Guide to Wilderness Survival.* New York: Berkley Books, 1983.

—On proof of past lives:

Bowman, Carol. *Children's Past Lives: How Past Life Memories Affect Your Child.* New York: Bantam Books, 1997.

ABOUT THE AUTHOR

Christopher Burford has a degree in electrical engineering with management school training. He works full-time as a senior electrical engineer and conducts workshops, healing, and readings in a part-time practice.

Visualizing aspects of the electrical power phenomenon, such as magnetic forces and current flow, is synonymous with his innate intuitive abilities. He has held management positions in the corporate world. Still practicing engineering, he aids people in awareness in his spare time.

Chris was led to a path as an intuitive in his childhood. Many experiences with personal energy, intuition, and the natural world honed his abilities and shaped his beliefs. He trained and completed personal work to become an energy facilitator, healer, intuitive, and psychic warrior. He is constantly learning new things about people and the universe. He believes that when working with people's energy, respect, honor, and integrity are paramount. Assisting people to reach their potential in life is his goal. All he does is a gift from a higher power.

Printed in the United States
By Bookmasters